LEADERSHIP GONE ROGUE

The Ascent Of The Economic-Terrorists, Religionomists And Moneyticians

&

The Descent of A Responsible God

ISBN: 978-978-558-664-0

ISBN: 979-864-007-615-8

DEDICATED TO

Clerics who have not yet sold 'the pulpit' to the highest bidders nor violated its dignity.

Politicians who have not yet attempted to exploit our ethno-religious sentiments nor bid for the 'pulpit'.

Journalists who have mastered the 'art of objectively' observing and reporting any unholy alliance between the pulpit and the money-bags politics.

Credo

I believe in God the Father Almighty, the Rational Creator of the universe. And in Jesus Christ his Son, Our Lord, who condemns empty religiosity. And also, I believe in the Holy Spirit, the Lord the Giver of Life, who empowers true 'religionists' to be the light and, not the darkness. But I do not believe in an irrational and irresponsible God of ill-religious people, whose mental attitude is both anti-religion and anti-rational; because he ceased to live or exist a trillion years ago.

Opinions are free but facts are sacred.

I don't call thieves corrupt; just because I want to be 'air-worthy' or 'politically correct'.

A thief is a thief, irrespective of what he stole.

You don't have to like my expressions, but you can't deny the reality expressed.

Contents

Chapter 17

THE ENTRANCE (OF SECOND EDITION)

A lot of things have been said, and a lot of books have been written about the 'not-so-right' sociopolitical situations in Nigeria. Many of those books have stated what might be considered the 'bitter truths', truths nonetheless that many of the readers could not swallow because they are just too bitter for many to swallow.

Sadly, it seems many (Nigerians) people don't like to hear the 'hard and sincere' truth. We prefer to listen to the sweet and soothing words and rhetoric of those who use high sounding words and religious semantics to deceive and steal our collective patrimony from us. If that is what you are looking for, then this book is not for you.

We cannot deny that our people's poverty and, of course, their religious and ethnic sentiments too, have been consistently manipulated by the elites across the board.

The northeast is a typical example of this. While I do not a hold brief for the 'northeasterners' or speak for the government, nevertheless, from my frontline experience as a soldier of Christ (and a 'defender' of my nation), I can say without mincing words that, if the politicians had not exploited the poverty and ethnicity of the people and the religious elites had not fed on their strong but, unfortunately, naive religious sentiments, there probably wouldn't have been the sad and agonizing 'phases of Chibok and Sambisa' in our experience as a nation.

But it happened, because they did exploit people sentiments, the rest is now history.

Thus, it is refreshing to find a son of the faith and of the land being bold enough to point out the abuse, misuse and misapplication of religion in Nigerian political terrains so succinctly without any disrespect to the faith.

The 'hard' fact of the hypocrisy of the religious Nigerians, who are, arguably, 'the most religious' people on the earth, is well presented by the author in this Second Edition of LEADERSHIP GONE ROGUE as he reflected on the level of the rot and corruption in our political and religious terrains.

It is indeed an honour to be associated with this work. Words well said, truths well presented, research well made, and facts well laid out.

If only we are a nation that listens to the truth and acts upon it, maybe our 'religious truths' would have helped us build our nation up to its great potentials instead of dividing us and making us the laughing stock of the world. This is a great work indeed. Well done.

Lt (Rev Fr) Christopher Oluwafunminiyi Odeluyi

Our god seems so jobless and irresponsible that he occupies himself with thinking for a people he endowed with efficient problem-solving mechanism - our brains….

Chapter 1

RELIGION GONE ROGUE

Religion is an indisputable fact of human experience; a genuine human phenomenon. Thus, in every age religion has been an important feature of human society. Whether we call it historical or non-historical or new age religion, its basic quest is simple: the search for the true answers to the ultimate questions of life, as well as making man happy. Even in those societies referred to as atheistic societies[1], evidences have shown that there were prevailing beliefs in some things, beliefs espoused by many in such societies that had control over their interests, emotions and mental states.

And so, religion, if properly channeled, has far reaching effects on the minds of those who hold it, and these effects can transform a people into progressively developing nation[2], since honesty and justice will prevail in such society.

However, the attitudes many of us –both the leaders and the led- put up in almost every aspect of our lives, are flavoured with a confused and frustrated understanding of religion. So, the god of our religions is perpetually burdened with the responsibility of doing virtually everything for us. Therefore, almost no room is left for human efforts, even when it is quite obvious that our innocent god has done his part of the deal.

The impression we, I mean most Nigerians, give ourselves or any keen observer is that whatever we do is determined by the god(s) of our religions. Why, because worshipping him in everything makes him happy. Thus, whenever there are challenges, it is considered his responsibility to leave whatever he, our god, is doing and respond to our distress calls, by attending swiftly to our demands, desires and problems. What a pitiable people are we! And what an over-burdened being, our god must be!

In fact, this god of ours is responsible for everything. He is responsible for who becomes our boyfriends and girlfriends, wives and husbands and, how many times we have sexual relations. He determines how many times we shall abort any unwanted pregnancies? This god is responsible for who becomes our president, governors, local government chairmen, councillors, commissioners, heads of street hawkers and market women associations. He determines the chairmen of anti-graft agencies and leader of treasury looting individuals in government and all affiliated corporations, the list is almost endless.

Our god seems so jobless and irresponsible that he occupies himself with thinking for a people he endowed with the most efficient problem-solving mechanisms - our brains and our minds. He provides money for a people he endowed with some of the most unrivalled human and material resources on earth. I won't be surprised if we expect him to brush our teeth for us, though he graciously gave us hands. What a country! What a people! What a pity!

This god of ours must be irresponsible, otherwise, he would be busy doing something better elsewhere, especially in those materially and humanly less endowed countries that are making a serious effort to task their brains and put things in order. After all, there are more than 7billion humans on the earth surface, and we are far less than three per cent (about 200 million[3]) of that huge sum. Yet, we and our nation are over-endowed with what could make us a great people had we chosen to.

Nevertheless, the irresponsible religious orientations of many of us, spiced with our negative ethnicism and the spiritual somersaults, have made it quite easy for the polithiefians, economic terrorists and religionomists to tap into this self-imposed bondage of deterministic religionism and recklessly exploit the 'crude oil' of our lives, while we are left with psycho-spiritual, politico-relational, and socio-economic environmental degradation. And like the over-abused and under-developed but handsomely oil-endowed states of Niger Delta[4], this deep exploitation of our life has made life almost not worth living for us, within the shores of our own abundantly rich fatherland, Nigeria.

Thus, a religion that ordinarily should be a tool of liberation[5] has become a tool of oppression and exploitation by the moneytical class and their religionomic partners.

This exploitation is fuelled either by our fanatic-ignorance, or the irrational refusal of most of us Nigerians to be liberated by an intelligent God of the universe and not kept in seemingly perpetual servitude by an irresponsible god of our own making. As a result of this development, many of us Nigerians seem to have unconsciously (or perhaps consciously) created and developed different gods, irresponsible or jobless gods that are different from the All-Intelligent Universal God.

Although all of them are erroneously mistaken for the Real, Rational and Responsible God of All Creation. Otherwise, how do we explain the relapse into national ethno-religious madness that we see these days, in spite of our impressive level of education?

"This is end time" or "There is God'' or "God will help us'' or "God dey" is almost always the preferred response of most of us to situations that should have been challenged by active condemnation of politico-economic gladiators, and/or to organize non-partisan peaceful mass protest against the polithiefians and their associates. If for nothing else, at least to show our disapproval to their flagrant abuse of power and economic rape of the nation by political elites and their insane cronies, especially (those) clerics from 'hell' who eat at their tables.

We, says Wegiel, may not have the power to prevent every act of injustice but we must not fail to protest against it. Of course, this statement, as far as our exploitative leaders and many of us in this context are concerned, is not true because "God will help us". Amazing! Who is fooling our visionless leaders or we, the followers, whose brains, it seems, are behind our heels?

The problems in and with Nigeria seem to be increasing. Sadly, however, the god we[6] claim (that he) directs our lives and gives us leaders, leaders who are, unfortunately, totally bereaved of ideas, appears to be getting farther away from our noisy and irritating 'god help us-ses'. Of course, that is if this strange god was ever near in the first place. At least that is the impression I get from our frustrating and often confusing religionism, as far as our life as a country is concerned.

Our politicians, religious leaders and economic-vultures have realized this orientation of our people, people who have refused to come out of their self-imposed unrealistic and frustration-ridden understanding of the *modus operandi* of the true God of religion. We have refused consciously or have been unconsciously conditioned, not to understand how the real God of a real religion relates to and with his adherents. And they, religionomists and politicians, are carelessly exploring and exploiting our sick understanding of God-man relationship in Nigeria's tragic drama of god-does-it-all –a sort of an endless Nollywood series.

Like any religious thinker, I affirm God's power but disagree totally with a servile understanding of this divine omnipotence, especially as projected by our crazy, bishops, evangelists, prophets, pastors, priests, imams, mullahs and sheiks, no apology sir.

God has his role and man has his. These two distinct roles MUST not be confused with one another. Man is not an animal that he should expect God to do everything for him, in spite of the huge mental, psychological, emotional, theological, philosophical, scientific and other investments he, God, has put in and on the man-project for his on-going advancement.

Even animal does the animal *basics* by itself before expecting help from outside of itself. Obafemi Awolowo, Nnamdi Azikwe and Tafa Balewa must be turning in their graves by now; I hope they are not cursing us as well.

We are materially rich, as a territory and land. Yet we are among the poorest people on earth. 'This is somehow confusing; how do you mean?' You may ask, and I will simply say, Shush! Take a breath. Think deep. Then, ask the gods or simply challenge our exploitative-leaders for explanations, this is not Saudi Arabia or North Korea or Burundi or Uganda or Macron's France. This is Nigeria, the supposed brain of Africa.

However, the question, I think, we need to ask ourselves, is, 'what is the problem with Nigeria: God or Nigerians and our pocket-thinking-visionless leaders?' The question above is what informed my reflections in the pages of this book. And I did this by deploying every realistic intellectual tool necessary -existential, political, philosophic, theological, sociological and psycho-spiritual.

Of course, this is not one-book-answers-it-all, no. My most basic interest here is to look at one of the most influential yet grossly overlooked reasons for our multidimensional and offensively oscillating stagnation –i.e. our servile religious mindsets.

In other words, I am looking at our funny deterministic religionism from another lens and, taking a quick look, too, at negative ethnicism and how the psychology of these two phenomena affect other facets our national life negatively.

I seek to please no one in the pages of this book and I have no apology for the thought expressed. Opinion is free but facts are sacred, so says an undying journalistic aphorism.

My intention, therefore, is to prompt us to ask ourselves more questions than we are used to. And to remove each layer of some areas that have something to do with the poisonous cup of the *wine of religion* brewed and packaged in Nigeria. Brewed and packaged by economic-terrorists, religionomists and moneyticians bottling company[7], a company whose primary interests are money, power and fame.

It is my humble duty, as much as it is the duty of every Nigerian whose generation is being wasted by our sightless leaders, to open the eyes of those who might have been blindfolded by their hyper ethno-religious sentiments at the expense of their effective involvement in the political and economic process of a truly holistic nation-building.

Or at least to challenge those who have been paralyzed by their ignorance of the very God they think they relate with, within the context of their intellectual-kwashiorkor drenched belief systems, so that they search more earnestly and see more clearly.

And also, to bring to the consciousness of those who have unconsciously fallen into the retrogressive mental-ditch of negative ethnicism (racism, tribalism and other primitive arrogant and ignorant '*isms'*), and the noisy *God-will-help-us* daily lyrics without knowing it, in spite of their education, advanced skills and seeming intellectual heights or higher knowledge.

To be honest with you, the reflections in this book was written with a scything-pen and it's razor-sharp.

...in fact the designer made sure he put a principle or set of principles in place to guide everything he designed, in other words, there is an order or law by which the universe was to be governed, and by which it is being governed.

Chapter 2

GOD OF THE UNIVERSE IS AN INTELLIGENT AND RESPONSIBLE BEING

The massive information available to us from the centuries of intensive scientific[1], philosophical and theological investigations at different levels (of these fields) has proved that the universe is a well-ordered system. It has been thoroughly designed, planned, organized and executed and still being executed flawlessly.

In fact, the designer made sure he put a principle or set of principles in place to guide everything he designed. In other words, there is an order or law by which the universe was to be governed, and by which it is being governed. What an intelligently responsible being could have done or planned this? The being that structured the universe[2] must be an intelligent and responsible being.

I am not concerned with the theological, philosophical and scientific arguments of whether it was a being or a group of beings or mere accidental cosmic forces that brought the universe into existence, or whether it happened 4.5 billion years ago or 900 million years ago or just 600 thousand years ago. I am rather taking all that for granted, and I am saying whatever or whoever was responsible for the creation or the invention of the universe (of which this peopled planet earth is a part), or whatever the name with which to identify that being is not my target here.

All that concerns me is the fact that that being, as a matter of necessity, exists. And he is obviously intelligent and responsible, judging by what we see in this enormous and gigantic artwork called the universe of which the earth is one of its major subsystems.

The order in creation is rather too obvious for any right-thinking person to deny or claim its creator does not exists. The intelligence of the creator-being is seen both directly and indirectly in this systematic artwork of creation. Let us take a very simplistic look at this planet earth for example, and we will see that the sun has always risen from the east and always sets in the west and, this rising and falling of the sun, to a great extent, determines how (a whole) lot of things are done in the animal and humans worlds[3].

The days and nights are determined by the movements of the sun. Days, weeks, months and years are determined by the east-west movements of the sun alone, even in the regions of the world where systems of counting days, weeks and months are based on the sighting of the moon -lunar calendar, we can still see the effect of orderliness in creation at work and, the intelligence of its creator.

The being that created the world must have had a plan for his creation even before creating it. Its structures, its multi-layered contents, the principles or laws on which and by which it would be run and governed. For example, IEEE, a merely human organization, will not approve any electrical/electronic device brought to it for approval, until its core electrical-electronic principle is mapped out. It simply makes no scientific sense to approve it without understanding its process. A process is an integral part of the scientific order.

So, the designer of the universe must have had a plan before creating it; at least from the human perspective, as an intelligent and responsible being, he could not have created anything in vain but for a specific purpose. Whether we know the purpose for everything around us right away by seeing or perceiving them, or discover them in bits and pieces over the years, centuries or millennia. The point is, there must have been a well-thought-out plan for his creation. The world he created for men to live in and all the necessities to support life are provided for men and animals alike, and indeed other forms of being.

In science, astronomy[4] for instance, the more the outer space is explored, excavated and probed the more things are discovered to exist without previous human knowledge of them. Even where there was previous human knowledge, advanced data and details are being gathered for further analyses. The sheer volume of data collected so far has continually amazed honest scientists and, make them even more enthralled with the amazing organizing force[5] beneath all they have discovered and (are) still discovering.

There are so many laws operating in the universe, no doubt about that. But these many laws are in fact under one supreme law of nature [6] which is the grand guiding law of laws in the universe. Laws or principles have been discovered and still being discovered or rather established in different areas of human endeavours, such as science and technology as a general umbrella for several other fields. However, to be specific I will say fields like chemistry, biology, sociology, anthropology, psychology, physics, aeronautics, philosophy, theology[7], pharmacology and all other scientific and non-scientific areas of knowledge. But these laws, in various scientific and non-scientific fields, are mere explanations or interpretations of parts of the eternally[8] immutable ground law of nature as it pertains to their disciplines.

There is nothing ever discovered by men, being discovered men or to be discovered by them that is outside the materials, forces or elements created by the divine creator-being and guided meticulously by the grand law of nature. It was designed solely for their operation, sustenance and control. Even as powerful and transcendent as spiritual laws are they don't always bypass the natural order or natural law arbitrarily, though there are exceptions.

Yet, natural law is sacred too. It is powerful and it exerts its presence always. For any living organism to stay alive and grow, for instance, oxygen and feeding are constantly needed. This is just natural, no matter how spiritual a person is this law will catch up with you if you dear to challenge its foundational principles.

It is important for us, therefore, to note that the designer of this universe, wherever his throne is, if he has any or if he can ever be pinned to a location, has shown by his own artworks in the universe – completed and ongoing- that he[9] is a being who cares for his invention.

A being of action, a being with a flare for well thought out plans. A being who respects his own laws, though not bound by them, and implements them with efficient immediacy where and when necessary.

He cannot but be intelligent and responsible, he leaves nothing to accident. Since he alone gives the absolute law that guides all in creation, and in us all he puts that drive to, loosely speaking, create and recreate something and to perfect that which we have created within the scope of the powers he has placed in us all[10].

There are different animals he created in the world. The lower animals, these he gives a somewhat fixed intelligence which makes them have a particular pattern of actions and reactions to and in their environments. He, however, gives the higher animals –i.e. human beings- an ever-flowing intelligence and thinking capacities which make them unpredictable. They are even more complex in their actions and reactions to their environments. Thus, humans are to, in the long run; take care of the lower animals and their surroundings and the environments both of them –man and animal- live in. Thereby sustaining both through the interaction of both species, human beings and animals, and of course, the environments of both.

Therefore, it goes without trumpeting it that only an intelligent being could have conceived, planned and continuously executed the complex systems and subsystems in the universe. Every matter and energy, place and location in space and time, whether on earth or in outer space, whether seen or heard or known to human beings or not, he planned them all.

The question you and I should ask ourselves is, is this creator-being the same Being our ill-religious people are worshipping with immense irresponsibility? If he, the creator-being, is meticulous in planning and executing the desired goal in an orderly pattern, why do many of us, his devotees, in Nigeria (and of course, elsewhere) find it terribly difficult to be orderly in planning our own society, especially in economy and governance?

If we believe he is the Lord and master of orderliness, why are we afraid of allowing the reign of the rule of law?

If he is orderly, why do many of his followers show the contrary in their daily dealings with their fellow country men and women?

If he is intelligent and responsible, why are those who claim to worship him often afraid of making decisions independently, and acting upon those decisions as soon as it is obvious there is a need for action?

If he is not some accidental force, why do our sick ill-religious and moneytical and religious leaders and their psychologically-challenged followers always hope for constant suspension of his laws in the name of miracles, when they refuse to use the brains he gave them?

These are questions that earnestly beg for uncomplicated answers from all the layers of Nigerian leadership and followership as well.

Nigeria and its people have been groaning in different self-imposed pains and groping in the darkness they have largely cast themselves in or cast on themselves, the list of agonies of Nigeria and its people is endless…

Chapter 3

A NATION IN THE WILDERNESS OF RELIGIOUS SERVITUDE

Nigeria and its people have been groaning in different self-imposed pains and groping in the darkness they have largely cast themselves in or cast on themselves. The list of agonies of Nigeria and its people seems endless. Realistically speaking, however, the geographical area of land called Nigeria is, in my own opinion, the best of the regions in sub-Sahara Africa.

Nevertheless, many of the people that feel its belly are the poisonous lot causing all sorts of ailments to its existence. The land is really green, as one of the Nigerian pop artistes, TY Bello, once sang. In fact, the land is not just green, it is freshly green. The land has abundant and unrivalled human and natural resources[1]. But then, we may ask, why are all these artificially engineered agonies, pains, poverty, militancy, homegrown terrorism, political and religious exploitation of all sorts hugging the land, as though they were created with the land?

Indeed many reasons can be responsible for our current experience. One of the most potent reasons often overlooked, however, is the aimless religious journey of many of the people of this amazing federal republic.

We and our leaders have continuously fanned the embers of religious deceptions into flames of aggravated spiritual illusions and militant material delusions. We and our religious leaders believe that we are so religious and prayerful that no nation prays like we do. Therefore, our God will do everything we want for us, when we want it and how we want. Our leaders dubiously quote passages after passages from the Holy Bible and the Holy Quran.

They twist their own consciences and those of the millions of us, their gullible followers, in order to accommodate their false interpretations.

These religious leaders, and the moneyticians who benefit immensely from their factory of psycho-religious deception of the people, continuously drive their followers to the region of psycho-mental barrenness and spirituo-material or spirituo-physical confusions. As result, we make ourselves slaves of our own environment without even knowing it. Consequently, we, you and I, are ready to take their words for the foundational truths on which all other structures of life are to be built.

They have created millions of individual wildernesses in the lives of many of us Nigerians. And they have made Nigeria into a huge wilderness groaning under the darkness of religious confusion which has helped us as a nation to progress backwards while other nations progress forward.

We have been assured consistently, by our religious leaders, of the presence and interest of God in our lives. In fact, they claim God is a Nigerian, in other words, he is one of us. If he is one of us, then he will take care of everything. This is how they deceptively induce their adherents to psychologically sleep off; hence they will not feel the pains of illegal economic surgical operations being performed on the lungs of our beloved nation.

Unfortunately for the people but fortunately for our religious leaders, the religious doses prescribed or administered to us (that is injected in our mind) through the syringe of false messages from their polluted pulpits across the nation, has made us fall into psycho-mental, spirituo-religious and socio-economic coma.

A coma or a psychology blackout that has left our numb religio-economic bodies at the mercies of 'our doctors' – the religionomists.

This wilderness of religious servitude in Nigeria is large, I mean very, very large. Although it is not physical its effects are just too visible to the naked eyes; therefore we really have no need of any magnifying lenses. There are as many churches and Islamic religious groups or congregations as there are religious families within Nigeria. Each one competes for space, territory and attention of everyone. Each of the religionomists devices efficient psychological, spiritual, social, pseudo-theological and economic techniques necessary for getting people, maintaining their 'loyalties' and remotely controlling their lives.

A *sound* student of elementary psychology and philosophy (or philosophical-psychology) will surely not find it difficult to understand that, he who has control over what you desire has control over you; at least to the extent to which you desire what he controls.

It is therefore not difficult to understand why they, the religious milkers (leaders), possess their followers. It is not rocket physics. It is a simple psycho-philosophical principle.

Anyone you possess (his or her psyche) you will dominate, anyone you dominate you will control, and anyone you control is your slave! 2+2=4, no abracadabra.

Our religious coma, as a people, has made us to be more scientific in our superstitions. Therefore, it makes our distorted understanding of the necessity of our active and physical participation in the process of socio-politico-economic change, growth and development at different levels very difficult and nearly impossible to correct. Religionomists drive us deeper into the state of psycho-religious coma because we allow them.

They tell us that they can heal all illnesses/diseases, solve all problems and challenges, and disasters are not beyond the power of their god to stop. Poverty will be removed from our lives once we follow them and their irresponsible god, progress will come our way when as a nation we follow their way or the way of their gods. And Nigeria shall be *a prosperous nation once again*, one US dollar ($1) may become less than one Nigerian Naira (N1) like it *was*[2] in the 70s and early 80s, if we do as they say. I suppose that's a holy day-dream from the realm of delusion?

In fact, they claim that because many of our co-religionists, their followers, pray a lot at different crusades, night vigils and congregational conventions, Nigeria will soon become a prosperous nation once again. Holy nonsense, what a deceitful people!

It is nothing but a holy deceit for anyone to say Nigeria will progress at the 'pace and dignity' a crawling giant such as ours deserves in spite of the ruthless and endemic political thievery and inept and purposeless leadership.

Our leaders are fond of shamelessly claiming god brought them to the office. Which God, the real one? No, it must be a god, and that god must be insane and grossly irresponsible, to see clueless people and prison candidates ascend the seats of power for no common good.

How can he bring them into power in an abundantly rich but poor country? Are we serious right now? So, he enthrones these national parasites and cogs in the wheel of our collective progress, then sits and looks down, and claps for them on his accursed cosmic throne? I don't believe such a god exists outside our brains or the brains of our leaders. If he does, he belongs to the depth of hell; I mean the hottest part of the everlasting molten magma.

When you watch these religionomists preach on the television and you listen to them on the radio, they beam emptiness and transmit blinding religious confusion with deafening deceitful scriptural repetitions. Each of them uses different psychological and pseudo-theological principles to win over more followers. Followers who become more confused about religion, God and their own *active consciousness in the Nigerian society* after listening to them, than they were before listening or watching them.

Even the most fundamental truths in the Bible or the Quran are intentionally or ignorantly confused with their own personal well-tailored, self-serving and properly designed schemes that perpetuate their life's desires – power, fame and wealth.

Every corner has a church or private Islamic congregation or shrines to some long lost deity. These religious houses are the laboratories where we develop our own versions of pharmaceutical products -that is fasting and prayer.

The religionomists are the lab scientists and medical doctors. These religious houses are our own versions of the factories of other serious nations around the world where cars, computer, TV sets, blenders, vacuum cleaners, spoons, plates, toothpick and other things are manufactured.

The religionomists are the factory engineers and factory workers, while prayers and fasting are the heavy machineries used in the manufacturing processes. Their adherents, on the other hand, are the consumers or buyers, and god is the sole supplier of the raw materials needed for production processes. What a wandering and confused people occupy this fertile but barren land?

We or rather many Nigerians are in religious slavery in a fertile but barren land. God himself is an orderly, organized and methodic being. A being who conceptualizes, plans and executes eternally, and in every man, he plants a spark[3] of his Intelligence, Will and Divinity.

These are powers no other being in the universe possesses except man and his offspring. Religious bondage is a terrible bondage because it uses two-prong approach - psychological and spiritual. When combined, these two tools are among the most efficient in manipulating any man, anywhere and anytime. Their effects on men have always been enormous.

Religious bondage can only produce what we are witnessing now in Nigeria. It is not new, different nations have experienced it at one time or the other, at different degrees and with different effects, even some are still experiencing it now as we speak. But many have made conscious efforts to be liberated and they have been freed indeed, or trying to be delivered completely.

It won't be out of place to say servile religious orientation was somewhat responsible for the reason Karl Marx called religion *the opium* of the people. Since he observed the dangerous effects of people's senseless attachment to distorted versions of the religion of his time and even the time before his, which in his view was not making them to take the type of radical step he would have loved to see people take against the established politico-economic order which oppressed in under the guise of the divine right of the leaders or lords.

We are, no doubt, in the wilderness, not just any kind of wilderness, but a wilderness of religious slavery. Metaphorically speaking, a land can be fertile but barren at the same time to the people who cultivate but who cannot eat of its produce. And also, a people can be free but be in bondage at the same time.

This is what I mean; let me illustrate this with a very, very simplistic analogy. A colonial[4] power imposes itself on a particular people. It seizes their land and controls their ways of life. It demands that they all cultivate the land without wages but it put (pad)locks on the mouths of everyone and fetters of iron on their ankles.

It enacts a law; 'no one takes anything from the plantations'. 'No one eats anything anytime without its agent's permission'. If they do, '…death is the punishment for disobedience!'

So they die in their thousands daily and hundreds of thousands yearly. Though, they are allowed to have enough rations to sustain them, not necessarily for the love of their lives, but so that they can work and farm its imperial plantations all over the nation, yet the rations were not enough to prevent starvation and death!

As far as these people in servitude are concerned, the land is fertile. Yes, it is fertile they know that because it is their land and they know it very well. But this land is barren now because everything that comes out of it and grows on it is no longer theirs.

Everything now belongs to the slave masters and to them alone. So, people can be free and yet be in bondage at the same time. Psycho-religious bondage is the worst form of bondage, since it places men under many imaginary boundaries and realities.

It tells you that the sun rises in the north always and sets in the south perpetually. It tells men you cannot and should not resist your leaders it is a sin, just pray for them, even though it is obvious that they deserve the purest of curses. If you disobey them, it is punishable by temporal and divine laws, even when it is obvious he is looting the nation dry. Hmm, well, I will say God Bless Nigeria, not its looters and those who rape it right from its youth and forced its brightest children out of its borders. Amen.

At different strata of the society we see men and women walk about, no handcuffs on their wrists and they are not imprisoned physically, but in their heads and minds, they are actually in Kirikiri Super Maximum prison.

They go everywhere with this prison in them, and being in prison is better than having prison inside you. We fear to ask our parents questions lest our god gets angry. We fear to protest against the government, even in the face of gross disrespect for our rights, so that we will not be arrested. We fear to ask our religious emperors questions that could have led to an important liberation in our religious cum economic lives. Why are we afraid? Well, because we don't want the god of the man of goodies to punish us.

We fear to walk in the sun so that we won't see our shadows which might be the angels monitoring us. We are afraid of night falls because demons might be lurking around the corners. We are afraid of closing our eyes because armed robbers might attack, even where no such threat exists!

What exactly is it that we don't fear, for God sake? We are neither North Koreans nor the Saudis that we cannot challenge this abominable madness flying all around in the cloaks of politics and religion. This is Nigeria, the supposed land of the enlightened minds.

The most powerful weapon to set anyone free from physical and emotional slavery, anywhere anytime, is the psychological freedom with an unyielding sense of self-worth. That is a sort of un-intimidated courage to seek for light in the dark and, not to get so comfortable with darkness which inhibits progress. Also needed is the boldness to ask questions, not necessarily to get answers all the time, but to challenge the intelligence of those who claim to know it all. Those who think only their minds comprehend all realities, even when it is crystal clear that they are losing their minds.

The most annoying thing is that instead of helping to set our people free, they are mystified more and more with confused religious (Muslim and Christian) congregational gatherings, syncretic doctrines, sermons, night vigils, crusades, Egbe Alasalatu[5], healing services and all sorts of ill-religious religious nonsense.

We are in our millions being sunk into the ocean of psycho-religious slavery every day and no one seems to be concerned. Why should anyone be concerned when it favours the religionomists and the political elites? Many Nigerians have been driven deep into the wilderness that has made us more advanced in scientific superstitions while serious parts of the world are breaking new grounds in scientific researches and developments.

It is not the case that we lack the capacity to invent technologically beneficial processes and gadgets, of course, we have that capacity in abundance. It is just that the elites in each state of the federation may not have enough time to steal if the emphasis is on that.

Those types of projects are capital intensive and it is easy to know when billions are swallowed. Ajaokuta iron ore project in Kogi State is but one out of many examples of economic pits that expose our kleptocratic elites.

As a consequence, that capacity to re-invent ourselves as a progressive people is not taken away but seriously challenged or terribly crippled. Consciously or unconsciously, they have stealthily encouraged us to dump our problems and responsibilities on the laps of some gods on holidays in eternal non-existence.

For instance, Ebola was brought to the Federal Republic of Nigerian (the crawling Giant of Africa) through a man named Patrick Oliver Sawyer[6]. He came into the country through an aeroplane with almost no one knowing he was an Ebola-carrier. But immediately it was discovered and announced that Ebola was now within our boundaries, many Nigerians bombarded their waves with one of their shackled declarations, 'it is the punishment from God and only repentance and prayers can heal it!'

Amazing, religion is confused for magic, though we condemn magic but carry its concepts in our belief patterns and reinforced it with our actions and inactions.

If Ebola was the punishment of God because Patrick Oliver Sawyer loaned us the virus in Nigeria on July 20 2014, the punishment of whom was it when it was discovered in 1976 in the then Zaire (now Democratic Republic Congo)?

Punishment of whom was it when it ravaged Liberia, Sierra Leon and Guinea?

This wilderness will never produce anything meaningful, except a more susceptible people who may wander through life without even fulfilling any of their impressive missions, irrespective of their educational advancement.

This wilderness will groom, and is grooming already, a more religious people with an empty spiritual life that produces deceptively annoying spiritualities. This wilderness will even produce more religious slaves, as governments at various level of our national life tacitly support the expansion and sustenance of this dangerous servitude by patronizing the religionomists, and even financing some of their projects under various guises.

It is never the duty of government to build mosques or church or support in building them. If the people are empowered, they will build not only churches and mosques but bridges. Any government that does this in Nigeria is a thief, criminal, ole, barawo, onyeochi, psychopathic manipulator –people's enemy number one.

As long as this nonsense continues, there will be more confused and superstitious Christianity practised by an already economically short-changed population who just want liberation at all cost. Regrettably, though, they are now caught up in the web of slavery that is subtle yet worse than we know it –it is psycho-religious.

And there will be more syncretic and fundamentalistic versions of Islam professed by another huge section of the Nigerian population, especially in the poverty-ravaged North-eastern states. A myriad of other religions, including traditional religions and even the so-called new age religions imported from everywhere, will try to carve out a sphere of influence in our already religiously psychotic, spiritually empty, psychologically possessed/depressed, socio-economically dominated and politically controlled life.

The effects are obvious already. A nation wandering aimlessly in the wilderness created by lifeless versions of religion; religion invented and reinforced by the religionomists and their affiliated bodies. This version of religion is generously accepted by the economically and, somewhat, politically oscillating people.

What do we see in the final analysis? What we see and get eventually is that a distorted and psychotic-religious-ideology[7] is now a substitute for sound economic and political empowerment, quality education and a better life for us the people; the true constitutionally recognized owners of this Blessed land of Nigeria.

…so the airwaves are bombarded with religious publicity stunts and marketing strategies of different categories, some poorly conceived and produced, some are a bit standard while others are just exceptional from conception in the studio to execution on air…

Chapter 4

QUESTIONING THE BASIS OF NIGERIANS' RELIGIOSITY

There are different religions or organizations of religious flavours in Nigeria but Islam and Christianity have the largest congregations or followers. Nevertheless, the versions of Christianity and Islam that dominate individual lives of their adherents and, of course, the national scenes are largely burdened with spiritual confusion, psychological manipulation, economic exploitation, religious showbizm, political sell-offs, rebranded paganism, title crazy and fame seeking of the power-conscious God-executives[1].

This, of course, is never a wholesale Nigeria problem alone; other nations have their shares too. But I am concerned here about my dear Motherland, Nigeria, just as the Chinese, Americans, British, Ghanaians and others should worry their heads about their nations, if they think their leaders are becoming rogues.

Their (i.e. God-executives') product-like religious services dominate our religious scenes. They are designed for marketing their so-called spiritual exercises[2] on the airwaves, and so the airwaves are bombarded with religious publicity stunts and marketing strategies of different categories. Some poorly conceived and produced; some are a bit standard while others are just exceptional from the conception in the studio to the execution on air. Whether you welcome them into your living room or not, they always find ways of invading your living room without your invitation.

They don't need your invitation anyway, all they need is the airwave that passes through your signal receivers in the corners of your home.

What are they selling and who are the primary targets of their products? Religion is our commonest product in Nigeria, no doubt about that. Of course, that is the opium of the people generally everywhere in the world, anyway. However, the primary target of the marketers of this opium is the religion-addicts, the people with illusion-infested minds and delusion ravaged religious orientations.

Put simply, they sell religion of Abracadabra from a god of confusion to refuge seeking Nigerians, a god that protects them from everything else except their exploiters and their self-imposed ignorance and illusions. We are such amazing people. What a pity!

Everywhere you look you must see a religious house. Every typical Nigeria major corner you turn you will either see a healer or a seer; a prophet or a sheikh; an imam or an ifa-priest; a spiritualist or an apostle; bishop or reverend; a pastor or an evangelist; a guru and/or may be 'Satan' himself (who knows?). In short, every corner has its own religion with its spiritual mediator or the god-executive[3].

There is religion everywhere in the land with little or no spiritual growth, so much religion yet little improvement in moral value, noisy religious gatherings everywhere but the crowds are empty of integrity just like their gatherers. There is so much religion from the highest places of authority to the intermediate and the lowest places of authority, and yet there is little or no love of the masses.

For their love is for their pockets, their god resides in the stomachs and they glory in their shameful exploitation of the masses[4].

Religion is the best selling product in Nigeria today and the producers of this product are really rich, connected and therefore have control over the lives of their followers. Of course, it is not called control, it is called 'the anointing'[5].

One can only wonder about the real reason for the types of religious trees that flourish in this country. Is religion, as embarrassingly practised in Nigeria now, still genetically connected to the universal primitive mind in relation to religious beliefs?

In plain English, is it an attempt to control the forces of nature/life? Can it be an expression of genuine devotion to the supreme deity, God? Is it a channel for letting out depression and other fears that assail our inner beings?

Can it be an attempt to escape the biting economic-terrorism in the land? Can it be a mere castle of illusions that give us false hope, hope which has kept us going nonetheless?

What is the foundation of this (informally) second most booming economic sector in Nigeria? Maybe you have the answers to all these questions. That is if you do not succeed in raising more questions yourself.

Religion, no doubt, is a universal phenomenon and it has been an integral part of human society for several millennia now. It liberates when employed properly, and enslaves when misunderstood and misapplied. However, many societies, the world over, have gone and grown beyond the primitive emotional attachment to religion. Religion has been put in its proper place and proactive scientific researches and technological advancements are given their rightful positions in the schemes of things, too, in order to continue the work of creation.

If you employ the services of anthropology[6], philosophy and psychology in analyzing the development of the phenomenon called religion; it will become clear to you that early man showed devotion or reverence for his objects of worship (a deity or deities) for various reasons.

The most primitive and fundamental of these reasons, however, was the need for protection from the natural forces that confronted the primitive mind of the budding prehistoric society. Though theologians or religious thinkers, especially those of the so-called great religions, may argue that the impulse to worship the divine is an intrinsic part of the being of man, if that serves them well, for now, no problem they may hold on to it, at least for now. However, as I said above, the desire to be freed from the ravaging forces of nature made man to look for a higher being(s) that can be of help, that is, liberate and defend him from his enemies – the forces of nature.

This primitive psycho-spiritual motivating factor for holding religious belief has somewhat changed in many societies, and is still changing in many (other) societies the world over; especially those societies that have discovered the scale of the powers to do and undo many wonderful things.

The powers deposited in them by their maker, whoever he is or whatever they think it is; and more importantly, they have realized the more purified, rational and higher bases for venerating their creator(s). Though, the sense of incapacity or powerlessness in the face of some of the life's challenges such as death and natural disasters has not and may not leave man totally from generation to generation. It is, nonetheless, psychologically redirected or expressed in different forms by different people in different societies, depending on how much of their inner powers have been discovered and put to use for the good of many.

However, in present-day Nigeria, it seems people are really still having the prehistoric primitive and/or archaic religious emotional attachments which were and are motivated by fear of some strange forces, rather than the *elevated value of love and reverence* of the creator-being.

It is very probable that the marketers of primordial religious emotions in Nigeria have realized that education, as presently conceived in Nigeria or by some Nigerians, is pathetic and has really not changed the deep-seated prehistoric religious orientation of millions. This orientation, a naïve religio-psycho-emotive disposition, I call religious primitive-gene or primitigene in many of my dearest compatriots. The gene fears anything and everything that does not suit the man in the short run, even if in the long run it is the best thing to have come his way if only he can look inward to dig up those powers his creator has deposited in him.

Thus, the religionomists market their opium, a false religious expectation, which effectively stimulates the action of this gene in their victims or illusion-driven followers, thereby, making them more and more dependent on ill-religion to solve their problems, even the minutest of problems that simple reasoning would solve. They have dethroned God from his place in the lives of the people by seeing the devil in just everything that obstructs people's way; devil's name is mentioned more than they mention God's holy names. People fear the devil more than they respect God (I guess without them even knowing).

Two things must be considered here in order to understand the basis of our sickening, stomach-turning, appalling, nauseating and disgusting religiosity:

1. For the populace: there is a yawning spiritual gap in our lives and, economic needs and greed of some of us are very high and our religious fluidity is ferocious.

2. God-executives: these are very skilful religio-economic strategists; they are religious marketers. The grandeur which the market they create brings seems more motivational a force than what politics creates for our moneyticians and their bootlickers.

1. The spiritual gap, economic need and greed of the people and, their religious fluidity

The Spiritual Gap

We must know the fact that, there is a huge spiritual vacuum in the lives of many (not all) Nigerians created by a host of circumstances -religious and economic. This gap or vacuum is terribly wide, deep and noisy. Unfortunately for us, nature abhors vacuum or emptiness. Simply put, something else must fill all seemingly empty spaces, spiritual or temporal.

Thus, this absence of connection with our inner being or the divine being within or the interacting universe is a problem, because it makes it difficult for us to experience the proper fruits of being one with that inner being or the divine being within or the interacting universe. This inner being or interacting universe is the real manifestation of the presence of our creator at that personal level of God-man relationship. The resultant effect of this disconnection is to constantly seek anything or anyone that tends to have a manifestation of this divine essence we lack within, even if the person claiming to be a messenger is a fox and a viper in the cloak of holiness.

This is one of the main reasons that make many of us, especially the leaders, to look very religious in words and in their noisily appalling externalism. However, when it comes to the deeds, the story is different.

On Sundays in our churches, we sing praises, not all our songs go for praises anyway, some are pure curses. And on weekdays at our crusades on open spaces and public arenas, we shout out our souls and call people to repentance. What about our noisy cast-and-bind prayer sessions in revivals and night vigils and other religious services? Yet there is a disconnection between the religion we profess and the lives of many of us. There are just too many ill-religious activities for me to waste the tip of my pen listing here on this page.

And for their Muslim counterparts, the story is not even different, if not worse. We, too, are very religious in terms of empty externalism; gestures that lack the purest of intentions required by the Almighty Allah. Five times a day we go for public prayers and on Friday we go for the Jamaal service. We fast like prophets and live like angels during Ramadan, though after Ramadan the devil is holier than many of us. We go for various Islamic religious gatherings, even on Sundays for special Islamic prayer services and preaching sessions.

Our women and ladies cover their heads with military obedience but open the borders below their waists to 'passers-by' with much mutual hospitality. I guess that charity is pleasing to Allah?

For many of us men, we carry heavy prayer beads about and do other *se-kaa-rimi*[7] acts of religious allegiance, but not even one of those goes beyond that externalism. We don't mind sacrificing the good of our immediate community for ephemeral political and economic gains. Gains which never really turn us into the overnight millionaires we had erroneously conceived before selling out our community to the highest bidders.

Fundamentally speaking, the spirit is actually not residing in the inner chamber, and this makes a lot of us religionists to adore those who claim to carry the message of the very *Being* we are disconnected from with much irrational but understandable passion.

Economic Needs and Greed of The People

Other factors that stoke the fires of empty religiosity of many of us are the economic needs and greed of many. Though, our government officials will always tell us that poverty perception is what is high not real poverty; if it serves them well, let them hold on to it. Sincerely and realistically speaking, however, many of us are wallowing in alarming poverty compared to the wealth of our nation and the opulence in which the looters live. We don't need to be told we are materially poor or rich to know what the economy is reflecting.

We know where we live, we see what our pocket shows us and hear what our dinner table says. We live in penury-designed semi-detached duplexes, which are built by destitution in the exotic, serene and peaceful but chaotic estate of hardship and misery. Ours is a state of insulting contrast.

We are among the richest nations (with the largest economy among the black nations) in the world. Yet, we the people are among the world's poorest. Isn't it ironic or confusing?

This mansion of squalor is protected with a powerful perimeter fence made of impoverishment, bankruptcy and insolvency. Many of us live in hell while on earth. No one really cares whether we live or die; in fact, we irritate our leaders turned looters who really would have preferred we all die once and for all. But who will worship them and their abominable offspring, if we are all dead? Therefore, they want our 'suffering and smiling' lives around but outside the damned highbrow areas, they live.

With this reality staring us arrogantly in the eyes, is it wrong for the millions of honest but poor to desire someone who has the magical wand? Well, I don't know. Anyway, it is not called a magical wand, no, that is not what they call it, they call it anointing. It is all about packaging, even when these angels are doing religious internet marketing and ecommerce, they call it evangelization. It is all about packaging, the way to hell is rebranded.

Yes, anointing is the name of the imaginary magical wand, so the poor[8] seek those God-executives who have or claim to have the magical wands or anointing that can give them hope. No matter how unrealistic and misleading this hope may seem to you and me, it is realistic for the man with no one to care for him.

He is rejected by his elected officials and unfavourable economic system scorns his very existence. But the religionomists are smart, they see dual uses for him and so they incorporate him into their empire. He will pay back at the appropriate time. This contributes in no small measure to the largely senselessly festering religiosity of most Nigerians. Of course, there are many generous real men and women of God out there, but to us they are the old school priests, imams and pastors, so they don't have the magical problem solving 'wands'.

Economic greed, too, has really added a huge number of other people to the moving bodies we see every day in different religious organizations, which dominate the national life of our most blessed Motherland. This category of people has enough to cater to their immediate needs and, with time (if they follow the normal process of life within a short time) their wealth will grow. But they, too, want to live like moneyticians, economic-terrorists and those God-executives we see around who spend lavishly and senselessly.

Yes, their problem is not lack but impatience and greed coupled with the reigning spiritual gap. And that is why they look for God-executives who can turn around their already growing fortunes. Or to inject the athletes-of-their-progress with performance-enhancing drug[9] that gives them edge over others abnormally.

Did you say banned substance? No, that is not the name; it is called miracle or divine intervention; that is what we call it. How truly divine is that? I do not know, don't ask me, the issue is that their concern is the result, not the process or agents involved in the process. This group of people looks good, educated and seemingly enlightened on the surface but beneath that smooth surface, they are psycho-spiritually at the level of the primitive inventors of religion, the *homo-religiosus.* Religion is not for them a love infused adoration of the supreme God for his majesty, but a fear-and-incapacity-engineered religionism.

Unprincipled Religious fluidity

And the third reason here is the deep-seated lack of doctrinal, religious and spiritual discipline[10] of we the people, which make us senselessly and irresponsibly fluid in the religious context. Like birds, we fly from one religious tree to another looking for 'only God knows what'. Our religious allegiance is but for a fleeting moment. In other words, we really do not see anything wrong in moving from one religious house to another, at a snap of the fingers. 'It does not matter what they do there, so far it soothes my interest', that is our simple spiritual-theology.

No basic intellectual questionings, which could have helped to solidify our mental state on the unyielding ground of rationality and religious discipline. The foundation of fluid religious allegiance is purely materialistic and incoherent or lame thought pattern. And from the point of religious and spiritual maturity, one of the worst things that can happen to a people is to have rationally watery, spiritually empty and noisily unstable religious discipline and allegiance.

No wonder somebody can change his religious house as often as he or she deems it fit, especially if a particular religious house has more swagger or packaging than the one s/he is leaving, irrespective of doctrinal emptiness, ideological illusion and spiritual delusion of the new one. There is something deeply wrong with our religious allegiance.

It somewhat reflects the fluid pattern of traditional religious allegiance, which allowed the ancients to move from one shrine to another without a second thought. I am of the view that there seems to be an unconscious attachment to the ancient African religious orientation. Or let me put this way, it seems we have psychologically transferred the mindset of the ancient religious inter-shrines fluidity into ourselves now and, spiced by a current decaying moral value system, array of political confusions and rising religious eclectism, we relapse quite often into that state of mind -innocently or naively.

In other words, we have now become members of new religions, but the deep-seated orientations of our forebears which saw nothing wrong in moving from shrines to shrines remain. For our (ancient) ancestors moving from one shrine to another is no big deal. Searching for what, probably, was not lost in shrines other than theirs was not wrong, since all deities are messengers of the Almighty.

This form of 'unprincipled' fluid movements was right and very correct then, and rightly so because their context and world view was different from ours. But not now, we must know where we (want to) stand. Except, of course, if we are saying nothing much has changed from then till now. This *religious-anything-goes* orientation has been dug up through various means, one of them being a section of the Nollywood[11]. Its emphasis on (projecting) fetish-syncretic mental attitudes in home movies, has, in no small way, carried over to the present age of economic crisis that subtle but 'revolutionary religious hodgepodge'. It says nothing is wrong if you change your religious affiliation like your underwears.

I mean, it's a kind transference of religious/spiritual orientation (from the ancients to our days) which the current national value system of *anything-goes* is reinforcing aggressively.

If you do your personal research, too, starting with your family, you will be amazed by what you will discover among your immediate family, for the most part. They are only Christians and Muslims when things are going well because both –Islam and Christianity- are like social clubs these days. However, in hard-times of crisis or normal life procedural challenges, they are traditionalists, spiritualist, cultist or they are ready to join anyone that has the faintest shadows of solutions. This disposition, to a great extent, has helped the market for the senseless religiosity of the day; the sachet-water-like religiosity we produce and sell to ourselves. Oh! Forgive me, we thank God we are now exporting it other countries, it is Naija-made!

2. The Religious Marketers, The Market They Create And The Glory this Market Brings Them

The First thing we should know here is the fact that the religious marketers know and understand their environment very well. They know the religious orientations and the economic realities of their people. Therefore, they meticulously expand these orientations and feed our socio-economic-spiritual anxieties with more life, energies and blood. And unsurprisingly, the eventual result of these actions of religionomists is our continued demand for their products and services; we are healthy but, unfortunately, sick –irrespective of our economic class.

Examples of these products will look like these: Weekly Instant Miracles and Healing service; God of Automatic Answers in the Valley of Jericho; Prophetic Hour of Intervention; 7-day Fasting and Prayers for Good Husbands; 3-day Fasting on Mountains of Liberation; Instant Visa and Employment Opportunity Prayer Conference ; You Must Be Rich Today Prayer Session; God of Independence Marathon Prayer Service; Power Must Change Hand By Force By Thunder weekly prayer meeting; Lord, Get Me My Glory monthly prayer programme etc.

And examples of the services may include but limited to: Holy Spirit Conventions; Shekem Conventions; Goshen Conventions; Covenantland Convetions; Fires and Miracles Conventions; Islamic Youth Conventions, Muslim

Women Conventions; Jamatulai Islamiyah Arafatiah Nijirianataf[12] Jihad and Convention; Ifa National Congress and festival; World Council of Ogun Worshippers festival and Annual Initiation Ceremony[13]; the list is longer than the rail track from Lagos to Kano.

Our dearest religionomists package their products and services in manners that make them attractive and appealing to everyone. From the man on the street to greedy ones in state houses, and even sometimes to some critical minds. They hammer themselves and their products with effective ferocity, strength and intensity on radio, television, bus and car-mounted bullish public address systems.

They also use newspapers, larger than life-sized bill boards, handbills, T-shirts, face caps, unsolicited text messages, online web pages. All the above drive their messages deep into the subconscious minds of a lot of us, and into the consciousness of many others.

Thus, by consistently coming in contact with the advertisement gimmicks of these marketers of religion day and night, our people who patronize them have been somewhat conditioned to believe they are having problems the god-executives alone can solve. Why, because God has sent them. God? Yes, God, that is what everyone says. Do you doubt them?

Dey no dey argue dream (you don't argue someone's dream), so says a common Nigerian pigeon-English parlance. After all, the objects of your dream were seen by only you, no more no less. Even if it was clear, that those objects of your dream were mere economic-plagues ridden mental projections, they still were yours and only you could have seen them. So arguing with you will be an exercise in futility. Thus, to them, it is God that sent them but to me, it is arrant nonsense.

In the end analysis, their activities create a very lucrative, money-spinning and high-paying market that brings with it, a skyrocketing glory and honour. So, in order to sustain their control over their little 'republics and kingdoms'[14], they fan more embers of empty and terribly annoying spiritual-syncretism into flames of illusion-ravaged religiosity. The religiosity which in turn brings them more spiritually, doctrinally and morally compromised client-members, thereby widening the market every now and then through different tactics that look religious to the generality of the public.

Of course, with the exception of those who know that appearance is very deceptive, and so they always look beneath the surfaces of religious services these marketers of religion present to us.

Nigeria's drivers (moneyticians, economic-terrorist and religionomists) are reckless because they do not own the car and care less about its safety and the well-being of its perpetual passengers.

Chapter 5

LEADERSHIP BY ACCIDENTAL DESIGN

To be a leader in the real sense of it, an individual must necessarily and consciously invest in his psychic, psycho-emotional, mental and intellectual and, socio-economic powers and energies.

He must stoke the fires of these faculties constantly, consciously and meticulously. So that when he needs their flames to purify any contaminated or unrefined precious 'mental-elements' necessary for building up, they will not fail him. Or when he needs their flames for destroying unwanted internal and external thought-elements, or for illuminating his own paths and those of the people he leads, the flames of the faculties may not be dysfunctional, erratic or dead altogether, thereby disappointing himself and those he leads.

Since he expects it (leadership position) to come his way someday, therefore, he prepares for it even before its arrival and, or its eventual actualization. Leadership at any level in life cannot be fulfilling or successfully rewarding to the led, if it is thrown on the leader by external forces without the necessary inner self-propelling-acceptance and, proper psycho-intellectual preparedness of the person assuming that position of authority. No matter how little or limited the sphere of operation of that office may be. Even if the office one aspires to occupy is as private and small as (the office of) a husband of a wife and a father of two children; one must be prepared for it or else danger breaks-in at the dawn someday, somewhere, somewhat and somehow. Is that not true?

Therefore, the leader, having prepared himself for the position he anticipates, he assumes it promptly when it arrives. And like a professional bus driver, irrespective of all the deadly bumps or pot-holes that he might experience in the driver's seat, he is determined to take his passengers safely to the most secured and proper destination. A place that makes the passengers happy and, makes them forget about the hassle of the journey and praise him ceaselessly for his effort.

If leadership involves genuine mental and psychic readiness, deep-skin ability to guide, direct, or influence people for achieving best goal possible or common good, then all Nigeria has got is a leadership class[1] by accidental design.

Why, because less than five percent of the leadership class is really ready to assume a leadership position for the common good of all. Of course, they all look prepared because they have money to throw around. They have connections to fast track their epilepsy-infested crooked plans and wield huge, I mean really huge, influence over the lives of many within their spheres of control.

But a person with a huge pocket filled with money without the necessary preparation only makes an idiot out of a foolishly rich occupier of the position of authority. The reason is that he rules and ruins the state rather leading, guiding and coordinating all the affairs by attending to and welfare of the people of the state, in other words, the common good of all.

Figuratively speaking, Nigeria's drivers (moneyticians, economic-terrorist, and religionomists) are reckless because they do not own the car and so they care less about its safety and the well-being of its perpetual passengers[2]. After all, they have politically-advanced crash helmets, economic spine-protecting-gears and institutional air-bags specially designed for our reckless drivers. And, in case all of those fail, well-funded life insurance is already in place for them and their miserable-yet-unborn 'damnation' they call offspring. These are people who get in the driver's seat of this nation. Their sole interest is to show off that they possess the car (Nigeria) now or can ride it, not with the desire of taking the passengers on a smooth and safe ride, either to their desired destination or any other location that makes life worthwhile for them.

The Nigerian politicians and their miserable backers, the supposed leaders[3] of the people, are fond of saying: "it was my people who said I should contest, I actually did not want to contest". *'Oro buruku lenu eye'* as some Yoruba will say, it literally means '*what a senseless speech from a bird's beak'*. The only message which, unfortunately, is the most verifiable fact derivable from this sick psycharcinogenic[4] attitude-of-mind which most politicians deceptively carry about, is that that they are *leaders by accidental design*, a little worse than ruthless coup planner and executor.

If my people actually want me to lead them and, in truth, I know I am not a leadership material in that context, practical wisdom and integrity demand I let them know I am not interested, besides there other ways to offer beneficial service to the community if the intention is to be a servant-leader and, not a ruler of servants.

However, I may assure them of my (tacit or plain) support for somebody more equipped for that duty than I, at least for the sake of the people themselves and edification of integrity. Alas! In reality, they want those positions of authority as though their lives depend on them. Of course, lives of most of them depend on such positions. But sadly, they are ill-prepared for the responsibilities of their respective offices. They, nevertheless, eagerly expect the rights and privileges that flow from them.

Their interest takes over and it places the interests of the people of the state beneath the waste bins of their respective offices. Whether the country bleeds ceaselessly and writhes in pains, pains which draw bloody-tears from the eyes of the world community, because of their jaundiced-interest, our (fake) leaders care less. After all, it was their people who beckoned on them to occupy the office. Simply put, their objectives for occupying those offices are not yet fully realized, thus the nation may bleed more for the time being!

They think more of mere obligations than creative management. They are never ready for that office even as they occupy it now. They have higher 'degrees' and some even have PhDs and some are professors, but they lack that psychic or psycho-relational power any real leader anywhere needs to connect to the office he occupies.

Their emotional intelligence is nil, which means they are a disaster waiting to happen. Their psychological wave scanner is dysfunctional thus they pick up wrong thought-waves for the wrong purpose from the wrong section of the society.

Their socio-economic understanding is ultra selfish so the wealth of their family is supreme. Their mental and intellectual banks are bankrupt; consequently, every reported objective reality around their maladministration and incompetence is a sign that somebody hates them and their wretched tribes. They are in front but they are not the leader, they don't even know the way. Even if they claim that by staying in the front of the led they are using Fulani-herdsmen leadership style, they will still be wrong.

Fulani-herdsmen are tactical, focused and courageous in their field of operation, that is cattle rearing. They know what they are doing in the jungles among the herds of cattle. The herdsmen are not perpetually static at any position, not even at the rear of their herds of cattle. The reason is that many of the times they will go to the extreme sides of the herds to redirect the straying ones and be in front, when paths are not so certain or when they fear they might run into wrong paths. However, when the seeming danger or confusion is over, and the paths are plain or clear they return to any suitable position (for the most part, they stay at the rear) to charge their herds of cattle forwards.

They are, practically speaking, never glued to any position while roaming almost endlessly through the jungles, villages, town, and cities of Nigeria. They are fierce, thoughtful and tactical in that realm. Thus, they, our political class, fail leadership test woefully even by Fulani-herdsmen leadership standards which many of them claim is their canon of operation. The reason for their failure, by this very standard, is that they have no meaningful conscious investment in the faculties needed for tough terrains of leadership. The Fulani-Invest[5], that is, the psychological, psychical, mental, tactical, emotional and social training of their boys and young men in order to toughen them for the possible dangers of the jungles, or for any assault from the villages or tribesmen they may encounter on their journey through the wilderness while leading their 'colony' of cows and bulls, is unique. They were prepared for an important leadership role, though in the republic of herds of cattle and, maybe, roaming spirits.

Accidental leadership by design, the world over has never favoured any nation. It has brought more disaster to the people who have the misfortune of having unprepared leaders, successively. They occupy the office they know they will never meet its demands, and they do not even learn while on the job. Why, because they may never enjoy the excessive (booty of the) privileges and rights of the office if they dedicated themselves to learning and learning fast while on the job.

Besides, why do they have to worry (their heads) about investing in their leadership 'toolkits' when already in the office? After all, these office occupiers are fond of saying, "'God' is the one who chooses and 'our' people know that, too. Don't the people know?" This assertion of these miserable lots calling themselves leaders is widely held among our leadership class. In fact, it is like a religious dogma for a many of us, the people, too, who easily affirm it by saying, 'well, maybe it is the will of God'. And no thanks to the informal unholy alliance between the jungle class, commonly known as the political class and, the religionomists also known as men of goodies (actually, I mean men of god, i.e. the MoGs), but I prefer to call them the sanctuary thieves (especially Rogue Reverends and Scoundrel Imams).

This mentality, as described in the paragraphs above, among the gladiators in our national public life and among those of us who have made ourselves the spectators at the arena of this insanity, has reinforced, continuously, the destructive grip of the polithiefians and their cohorts on power and the machinery of the state.

Since, generally, everyone turns to God to beg for the change of heart of his unmerciful servants or to remove them altogether, instead of telling those that claim to lead us to do the right thing or get the hell out those sacred offices.

If it was in other 'climes' the people, through their constitutionally guaranteed right to freedom of assembly and to protest, will challenge their governments or politicians or leaders directly, even if those politicians concerned will lie effortlessly in responding to the challenge the people are reacting to, as they often do, they make sure they still respond anyway.

Nowadays, here in Nigeria, unlike in the past, we turn to God! If a road or something else is bad within the state in other 'responsible' countries, their governments are asked to do it by the voters (or taxpayers) who gave them the legitimacy needed to be in government. However, in Nigeria of today, we call our irresponsible god(s) to come down and fixed it. It is a pretty miserable reality in this land, and it is frustratingly annoying.

We cannot turn to the man in power because he never wanted to be there but gods put him there, so we should talk to the gods to remove him?

Unfortunately, the real God of the universe is not pleased with our false accusations. Therefore, he sees our attitudes as some sort of an insult and ungratefulness, to put it mildly, or blasphemy to put it plainly. Why, because in spite of our educational advancement our (I mean a lot of us, not all of us) lame or lazy and simplistic understanding of God's rulership over (the universe or) Nigeria is not just wrong, but almost extremely insulting.

God does not do for man what man has been, *ab initio*, empowered (through the actual grace of God) to do for himself by his strength. What God will do for him are those things that are naturally beyond his powers as man. Thus, the general pedestrian theology of seeing God as the king-maker when it favours those in power, and when the led are too lazy to ask basic questions or challenge the official narrative with necessary ‘melting point vehemence’, forcefulness and passion will only produce more spectator-footballers in matches they ought to be participants, active players I should say.

Let’s put it plainly, Nigeria will never run out of accidental leaders by design or leadership class with managerial sight impairment, people with no personal sense of direction or prerequisite mental, intellectual, emotional, psychological and psychical energies for leading a people and a nation of amazing wealth like Nigeria. As long as we, every man and woman, old and young, educated and simple citizen, *forget that God* has actually delegated the necessary or appropriate powers to determine one-billion-and-one things in the universe[6], we will never stop being led by accidental leaders, although we deserve better leaders. We do, indeed.

Dear compatriots, the powers to do are in us, the will to do is what is missing. Think about this, this is our nation and our motherland with the largest economy in Africa, and we are the most glorious and the most populous of African nations.

Let us use these powers in us wisely to challenge the official manipulative and exploitative narratives of the (current) office occupiers who pretend to be leaders and the (resultant) change will amaze us all.

However, whipping up religious sentiments in a subtle manner works really well. Yes, it does among a people who believe that their gods are eternally busy with nothing rational than deciding for them every time, what they must do, when, how and by whom it must be done…

Chapter 6

FOLLOWERSHIP BY ACCIDENTAL-DESIGN

A follower could be described as a devotee or supporter or disciple of a person or something. For you to follow someone or something in any rational, semi-rational or even pseudo-rational human society, it is expected that you have something that, no matter how infinitesimally small it may be, pricks your consciousness about that person (or thing) whenever his (its) existence crosses your mind.

In other words, to be a supporter or disciple of anyone or anything you MUST consciously choose to follow and/or obey the person or the principles of the person (or thing) in question.

In our context[7], however, that is not always the case, because of the pseudo *psycho-theology of helplessness cum god-will-decide* that rents the very air almost everyone breathes daily. The same mindset that produces accidental leaders by design is busy molding millions of followers that never really give their consents to being followers but since some jobless gods make it so, so they do the following because of such gods, thereby becoming accidental followers through or by design[8] of the gods and their detestable anointed ones.

Of course, there are myriads of issues in Nigeria that will make any right thinking person ask questions upon questions with the sole aim of finding solutions. But this problem of *accidental-followership-by-design* has always raised questions in my mind, and, whenever I raise this issue what I get in return, in most cases, can be summed up in two sentences: "what can we do, when we are not in government?" =equals= "Only god can save us."

It is sad, very, very sad that large chunk of the populace has the mindset that has consistently enabled the unfortunate, detestable and abominable political class[1] and its allies to marginalize and exploit us, day by day. It is not God's fault, it is our fault. Since we foolishly believe that we cannot do '***anything***' to pull down any undesirable element in power, after all, god[2] put them there.

However, January 2012 fuel-subsidy massive nationwide protests should have shown us that the real God, the responsible God of the universe, the real Intelligent God has never done and he is not doing and will never do for us what he has empowered women and men, old and young to do for themselves.

In addition, those protests also showed us or any reasonable Nigerian (I believe we all have our minds intact) who is not mentally-born-blind to know that we are too powerful as a people to be led by our noses.

We are too powerful indeed, if we made up our mind, not to be unjustly suppressed, economically and politically, by any illegitimate or legitimately-illegal regime, administration or government through the instrumentality of the demoralized, poorly remunerated and fun-and-life-loving Nigeria Armed Forces.

Don't forget that the members of the armed services have families, too, whom we are fighting for as well, *when they go shopping on the street sides and mami-markets where we shop too, they don't get anything* from the largesse of the office occupiers.

Besides, we are peaceful Nigerians asking for what is legitimately our right. Yes, our right from those 'illegitimates' occupying the holy public office for the good of the 4% at the detriment 96%. Isn't that a shame?

So, if they (men in uniform and their puppeteers) hurt the society more than bearable, then the country will go up in flames of more protests, *even more than protests 1993 and 1994 or the recent 2012 explosive protests that scared the hell out of Aso-Rock occupiers and their state minions,* and there will be a change of government by the real 'people' of Nigeria, not by any stupid divine intervention; but by You and I[3] –everyone burdened by their irresponsible leadership- and I don't even mean by useless, meaningless and destructive violence or any senselessly chaotic revolution (that is often counterproductive).

Let me ask you a couple of questions: why was the federal government afraid of our very national and explosive January 2012 pro-subsidy protests? And why did they hurriedly occupy Lagos with soldiers just because we protested? Where were the senseless and irredeemable gods of in-actions and cowardice when we decided to deploy our God-given right to protest? Were religious and political leaders genuinely in support of the people? Fast forward to 2018: across the spectrum, on whose side did the political and religious elites stand?

However, we seem to have been doubly bound by the most advanced fetters of iron made from a special iron-ore called *god-save-us-mentality* (opium of the people as Karl Marx called it). This is constantly and methodically reinforced in an aggressive but harmless and soothing manner by the religionomists – the agents of the moneyticians and economic-terrorists.

This pedestrian logic of we, the people, who are the accidental followers, may be summed up as this: *we do not want this man in power, but since we have no powers, not even our* collective will to oppose *him may yield any result,* then, *we cannot do anything only God has powers and only he can do something about him. We shall keep quiet to allow him (the man or god?) to do whatever he likes.*

Consequently, because the man in question knows that the predominant pseudo-life psycho-theology of the people is confused-and-defeatist, he buys his way into office with virtually no opposition from the people. Then while in office, he uses the machinery of the state to reinforce our prevalent confused and defeatist mindset. He achieves this by doubling his powers in various forms and tactically sponsoring and funding more religionomists[4] and several political opportunists, sycophants, and bootlickers.

Only God *knows how many times* I had to stop listening to some unfortunate, Mephistophelian and deplorable religious leaders in the pulpits, even within the so-called Orthodox churches, because, like the confused Evangelical and Pentecostal churches, they reinforce state manipulation of our souls. If the there is mist in the in the pulpits, then expect clouds in the pews.

Damn you all, you fake clerics. The pit of hell is still gaping. Religion is and must not be an extension of the state's manipulative programme.

Now that the man we do not want is in power, god must have put him there, or how else do we explain his emergence? So he goes to mosque or church in order to do dance-giving or tithe-dashing, cleric-buying-and-tying and sanctuary-renting. And the officiating imam or priest, pastor, reverend, prophet, evangelist, or whatever the hell he calls himself, strengthens the people's mental bondage and sells them even in their presence when he tells his congregation and the client-politician that:

Allauh Akbar... or Praise the Lord...Only god(?) determines who becomes a ruler because only him can decides who should see tomorrow. Therefore, whether the whole world decides they don't want you to be president of this country, if (since) god wants you god will still vote you in. And now god has done just that by making you our new president (governor, senator etc). You, Mr. President, however, has shown that you are a good Muslim or Christian by coming to thank Almighty Allah/Jesus Christ (and patronize our business centre?).

I want to use this medium to tell all of you (the people in bondage, here present)to pray for our (inept and illegitimate) president. And to always support him and listen to him because he is the god you cannot see...To obey him is to obey god and god will bless you in Jesus' name.../ Insha Allah....

The unwilling followers are now made to follow the so-called god-anointed by accidental design[5], because he, the man of gods (of money, fame, connections, and power), has given us both the reasons and orders to follow our oppressors turned leaders. Besides, the politician in question is our co-religionist (now?) and so religious sentiments take over and enslave our rational faculties.

Thus, by design we the people now follow those we would not have followed, which means the design is accidental. The political class and their collaborators, in this context, I mean the religionomists, who strengthen this destructive slave mindset of the people by deploying the most powerful elements of any religion: the psycho-spiritual principles.

Nevertheless, if only we, the people, could evolve that psychological freedom, a firm sense of self-worth, a real understanding of our *'inner divine powers'*[6] to determine our course in life as a people, and then believe in our own right to have a say in who becomes our leaders, irrespective of his religious taste, ethnic affiliation, political connections, and how deep his pocket is or what the national senseless gods of politics say; we would have built or be in the process of building the country of our dream.

We will then become *willing followers* with functional *politico-religious* and rational faculties to choose our own leaders through our God-given powers and constitutional guaranteed rights. And not some irresponsible men or women in the cloaks of god-executives who are destroying our lives by subtly supporting and choosing miserable and not-fit-to-live leaders for the already over-burdened and dejected populace.

However, whipping up religious sentiments in a subtle manner works really well. Yes, it does among our people who believe that their gods are eternally busy with nothing rational than deciding for them every time what they must do, when, how and by whom it must be done. Wow! It works like magic! The process is so self-lubricating and systematic that we rarely see this whole design, and our own contribution to its disaster-prone growth. We (arguably) unknowingly reinforce it with our active participation in this self-imposed slavery, by way of constantly seeing ourselves as spectators in a match we should be the players and even match officials in some contexts. No wonder, whenever we are told this *real but subtle* underlining current we will not listen. Or, worst still, we simply reject the message, shout down the messengers, and call them names instead of reevaluating our followership of the status quo that puts us in tight corners. What a class of followers are we?

It's a pity and a shame that we don't challenge our status quo.

God put you where? You may ask them a hundred times without any reasonably satisfying answer. God is now, a cheap scientific lying rod, used as an agent for authorizing and legitimizing irrationality of any kind within an irredeemably directionless leadership class, and intellectually lazy but senselessly religious followership.

Chapter 7

STAGNANT NIGERIA: WHO IS TO BLAME? GOD, INEPT LEADERS OR SENSELESSLY-RELIGIOUS AND POLITICALLY PASSIVE FOLLOWERS

There are at least four fundamental elements of any state in the world, and these are people, territory, the government, and sovereignty. The people are, in my view, the most fundamental of the four elements, but sovereignty is the most distinctive seal of independence.

Since it (sovereignty) asserts the supreme freedom of a particular people from another group; or put clearly, it asserts their liberty from every form of 'illegitimate internal manipulation'[1] of their common aspirations or desires and any form external control[2] by foreign powers or corporations.

The people, however, cannot live in the air, so they necessarily must occupy a space (territory) on land and maybe on the water. Besides, since human beings are among the class of animals that live in the community and the highest of them in terms of intelligence, it follows that they will need a coordinating agent(s) or government. Consequently, a *real* government always likes to affirm its independence from any foreign power or influence, and also from any internal element interested in subverting the will of the state for its selfish end. As a result of this, it invokes the principle of sovereignty or always asserts its independence by any means necessary.

However, when the sovereignty of the Nigerian state is threatened, economically and politically, to a point where the country is oscillating between an outright stagnation and a progressive-regression, due to the activities of a bunch of criminals in different exotic attires, whom do we blame?

When individuals with bogus titles and salaries legitimized by unjust ordinances and laws, whether they wear well-ironed suits-and-ties or nicely starched agbada and abariga, who do we blame?

Do we blame God? If we blame God we, will be judged by many genuinely religious people (anywhere on earth including Nigeria) as an ungrateful lot who, without verifiable reason, blaspheme against their creator.

And if we blame the people, they will tell you (in fact, that is what we have always heard from them) that you are biased and unrealistic in your assessment of them. "What can the people do?" I am usually asked, "except to pray that God should change things for good?"

My goodness! Is this a blame game? You can say that to the marines! Blame the pathologically retrogressive and directionless leadership for ruining the country instead of running it. It is that simple.

However, the 'ruinous elites' are quick to hit back at you, if are bold enough to step out of the line of the regimented thought-stream of the majority. They will either tell you, that you are jealous of their positions or tell you that god brought them into such offices and, god could not have made mistake in bringing them into the offices concerned!

God puts you where? You may ask them a hundred times without any reasonably satisfying answer. God is now, a *cheap scientific lying rod,* used as an agent for authorizing and legitimizing irrationality of any kind within an almost irredeemably directionless leadership class; and seemingly intellectually capable but politically lazy and passive and senselessly religious followership.

Do We Blame God/gods for Nigeria's Woes?

Who is to blame? If God, again and again, is used as both the battering ram and defence-shield, then who do you blame for the constant assaults on our collective wealth[3] and intelligence? Or who do we blame for constantly throwing a spanner in the works of our desire to move forward as a nation and have solid political sovereignty as a people?

If everything is always (deceptively) pushed to the doorstep of the (God?) god of religion, then, there is either something *ontologically wrong* with the god we claim to worship. Or we have tweaked our understanding of that (God?) god or our intellectual-data-capturing and reality-analyzing-mechanism[4] is malfunctioning or the three of them put together.

After a genuine examination of the hierarchies of authority in the Nigerian society; from the highest to the intermediate authority and from the intermediate to the lower authority, and from the lower authority to we the people, ourselves -both secular and religious- all I see, here and now, is an uncommon nonsense.

We wear a suit of moral bankruptcy, the tie of spiritual blackout, hat of intellectual manipulation, the shoe of social deceleration and psycho-religious epilepsy and, the (wrist)watch of administrative incompetence!

Since the hierarchies are riddled with bullets of ineptitude, thus the people suffer double tragedies of: (1) chasing after illusion while wearing the jackets of fear, shirts of confusion, ties of damned docility and trouser of home-grown slavery and; (2) we ride in high-speed train of self-destruction made with metals of ethnocentricity and equipped with advanced technology of beautiful but irrational religious-biases. In fact, a lot of us actually worship imaginary gods, unconsciously, in our daily living and not the Almighty God, I dare say. And God is, surely, embarrassed with our unnecessary self-deceptions.

So, what about the imaginary gods' challenge? Yes, they (the gods) carry the burdens of having to walk for their devotees gifted with strong legs but will not walk even in their fifties (Nigeria is 59). Think for their devotees with powerful but not-to-be-tasked-brains because they won't think with them. And act for their devotees endowed with multiple higher faculties, including the amazing intellectual faculty, yet they do not know how to act in any given instance of national political rape or incest against our nation.

So, I ask again who do we blame for the oscillating stagnancy of Nigeria: God, Inept leaders or senselessly-religious and politically passive followers? We may be in perpetual homegrown bondage if we do not stop expecting those imaginary gods, who are on the journey of no return far away from their ill-religiously able-bodied but politically lame creatures occupying Nigeria.

Many religionists have claimed that, due to our fervent prayers, Nigeria has progressed in every sense of the word. Well, deceptively speaking, that is right somewhat. But plainly speaking, that is, in relation to the wealth of this super rich but very poor nation -rich in terms of human and material resources- Nigeria has been oscillating between regression and stagnancy. Or to put mildly, we have been retrogressively progressive. Our progress has been in descending order, rather in the ascending order.

Although, religionomists, political opportunists and people like Dr Orji Uso Kalu, Bishop Oyedepo, Otunba Alao-Akala, Senator Iyiola Omishore, Aliko Dangote, Femi Otedola, Pastor Ayo Oritsejafor, Bola Tinubu, Dr Goodluck Ebele Jonathan, Dr Olusegun Mimiko, Ali Modu Sherif, Godswill Akpabio, Senator Bukola Saraki, Ladoja, Abiola Ajimobi, Rtd Gen Olusegun Obasanjo and many others like them, most likely, will not agree with the assertion that we are retrogressively progressive. That is our glorious days are seen in the past rather than in the present.

Yet, anyone who does not see the life of Nigeria with their jaundiced eyes and has the mental capacity to see black as black and not black as white, knows the truth. We are not where a nation of Nigeria capacities, potentials and size should be, simple. We should have been there had we chosen to. Many of our leaders are failure. Pure and simple.

God or gods, what do we mean when we irritatingly say 'God will help us' in a circumstance that needs just a simple proactive step or our ultra-sharp condemnations or mass peaceful protest, or even active involvement in the process and/or engagement with those in office? What does anyone that is above 18 years of age with, at least, average-intelligence[5] mean, when they say 'God will help us'?

If you take a deeper and systematic look at what many of us say when commenting on or explaining God's function, action or inaction in the prevailing situations in this country, you will discover that we actually have God on our lips all the time, but not completely in our understanding.

Our understanding and actions seem to actually portray gods or some ridiculous beings other than the real God. Why do I say we are unconsciously talking 'g' in a cloak of 'G'? Because we ask for divine intervention in everything even in crossing neighbourhood gutters. Thus, it makes no sense to believe we call on God to help us cross neighbourhood drainage when we just need to place a plank over it and walk across. The pain is in getting the plank and placing it over the gutter, not in walking across. So, we are simply deifying our 'inactions' in various senses and calling them gods while mistaking them for God in our understanding.

God did not create us by accident. Everything he created including man, the crown of his creation, was well-planned. An intelligent God would not want us to substitute higher divine qualities for animal level intelligence in the name of 'inactions' due to the cultivated habit of incessant fear of everything except God.

This is what I mean, let me explain.The Divine Supreme Majesty in whom we all have our beings, he who sustains all things in existence is an Intelligent/Rational 'Being' and he 'Wills' whatever he wants. These mental/intellectual qualities (will and reason) are the faculties of the spirit which is the life of the *soul, the* soul which is the principle of life in man. These are unique intellectual faculties which we share with God; no other being in the natural orders or planes shares these faculties with God[6], only man does.

To affirm the presence of these powers (including spiritual power) in man, God, according to natural reason and the holy books (Bible and Quran) of the two major religious traditions practised in

Nigeria, delegated the powers to determine the position of other beings in the universe according to his (man's) wisdom[7].

Thus, man is by divine design a little less than the divinities or the angels[8]. Therefore, ruling the world and all in it in the name of God has been decreed from the beginning of creation. In fact, those who have mastered these faculties fully have been able to manipulate many things in the created order and even beyond. There are those who manipulate invisible agents or explore their inner beings, too, to their own advantage. Why, because man is an elevated being among everything God created in this natural order.

He shares in the divinity of God; man has spirit (the divine elements in him) *and the spirit has two faculties 'will and intelligence'*. It, therefore, means that these two are divine qualities, freely given to man by his creator, God. You don't have to agree with the details of my analysis to see the truth as truth; the basics are undeniable, so stick with the basics.

Thus, this *eternally intelligent and free* (from any external force) 'being', has designed man to take decision for (man) himself and in His (God's) name and they will be binding even beyond natural plains. It is an indisputable fact that any country anywhere in the world where these powers have been put to use positively, progress and breakthroughs of varying degrees have been both their companions and their partners; even if many of them have been, by Chrislim[9] or Judeo-Christian standards, judged to be ungodly nations or pagan nations.

In my own view, therefore, I say without mincing words that The Divinely Rational and Self-Willing GOD, who created different orders of creatures but put (the) man in a uniquely elevated position, would not under any situation, circumstance or condition do for man what he has empowered him to do for himself. NO! It contradicts the principles of divine intelligence and natural rationality.

If he (God) must intervene it must either be because his (man's) *will and intelligence* have been so subdued that beneficial actions from him are almost impossible[10] or his *will* and *intelligence* no longer exist, probably, he is now seen to be at the same level with lower animals, therefore, it is impossible to sanely save himself or the situations around him.

In line with the above assertions, it seems evident, therefore, that the being whom we seek his assistance in most 'crossing-the-gutter' cases, is neither the Supreme Being nor a single being, but a college of beings woven out of either our suppressed (traditional) religious environment, or our hazy knowledge of the All-Mighty, Intelligent and Self-Willing God, or popped up by the prevailing economic frustration or combination of all the above.

Consequently, I say boldly here that God is not in any sense responsible for the oscillating stagnancy of this republic's honest, hardworking, simple but politically indolent people[11]. If any spiritual being(s) must be charged with our guilt or laden with our failure to move forward as a nation, or affirm the sovereignty of Nigeria and Nigerians against the wishes of the internal elements that assault it and the external elements that exploit it, then, it is not a being of intelligence that we must accuse but a college of eternally irresponsible beings.

Beings created by those who call on them, even while these invented gods are always on sabbatical leave or honeymoon in the sun where no communication signal -technological or spiritual- has ever penetrated.

Do We Blame the Leaders of Nigeria?

Who do we blame, if we cannot blame God? The leadership class in Nigeria cannot under any condition be exonerated from the woes of Nigeria. They are the technical designer, structural engineers and project supervising managers of the

Stagnancy/Retrogression of Nigeria Project (SR.NiP), and they have been efficiently professional in the execution of the project, and they have foreign partners in certain bankers and banks of the conceptual West[12]. The same West who always claim the moral high ground, even though they are the *agboode gba foo le Nijiria[13] and around the world as long as they benefit from the dirty dealings.* People don't loot their country's treasuries and take the proceeds to Asian or South American banks. No, they take them to the West –UK, Germany, France, USA, Canada etc!!

The leadership class is fondling with the testicles of the Nigerian state which is lying flat on the ground, exhausted and in pain; their joy is simple, the giant is under their evil control.

This means that the giant (i.e. Nigeria) has no functional will of his own while in temporary limbo, in spite of his huge but largely untapped energies, powers and strength. Since his hands are bound to the iron bar of political confusion, religious obsession and epileptic educational policy by those who should help him build his strength.

His legs are chained to the pillars of economic somersaults and directional blackout. He is covered in the cloth of acquired infrastructural deficiency syndrome (AIDS), scientific and technological superstitions, and industrial retrogression by those who should aid him in developing a powerful set of sprint techniques.

As if that was not enough, his neck is strapped to the (iron) bar of jaundiced national planning and policies, advanced insecurity of lives and properties, he is poisoned with pedestrian-ethnicity[14] propelled by those who should help him position his head to see far ahead of other nations. After all, he is an exceptionally handsome and enormous (state) blessed with unparallel height *but unlike Jesus who had 11 disciples 1 Judas, Nigeria (leadership class) has 11 Judases and 1 disciple.*

These class of clueless looters known as leaders find joy in challenging the sovereignty of Nigeria by stabbing this prostrate *giant* in the chest with razor-sharp daggers by looting of its treasuries with ease, while it bleeds continuously without any medical (economic) aid. The leaders (or looters) compete with each other to see who will emerge champion in the *Corruptlympic games* organized in Nigeria, through the help of their western partners and backdoor-inventors.

The medals (gains) of these *corruptlympic*[15] games are for our insanely looting (ruling) class, their collaborators and their abominable households. The pains of losing to them, however, are ours, the people of Nigeria. Think about how many of our finest 'brains' in any field of human endeavours that have been forced to look elsewhere for a home, even though their hearts have always had only one home, Nigeria.

Admittedly, these (corruptlympic) games are played the world over but the ruling class in Nigeria has one of the best star-studded teams (i.e. filled with individually talented 'corruptlympiaens'). They rule and loot with ease because god is always on their lips to cajole their god-fearing people who may kneel on broken bottles and razor-sharp nails if they are told do it in the name of god? Damned that god or those gods!

Those who occupy our driver's seats at various leadership positions (secular and religious) are too quick to adopt god as their scientific lying rod in the 21st century so as to cover their paralyzing ineptness, noisy emptiness, chronic visionlessness and horrible (dark) deeds.

For example, Governor of Zamfara State, Abdulaziz Yari, while commenting on the unfortunate-but-not-new outbreak of Meningitis on Tuesday 4th of April, 2017 was widely reported to have suggested that the outbreak was God's curse on (us) the people for the sin of fornication. "There is no way fornication will be so rampant and God(?) will not send a disease that cannot be cured…"[16], he was quoted as saying.

In fact, according to Emir of Kano, a prominent religious leader, the governor seemed to have given the impression that fornication is a Nigerian thing; so meningitis type C is the reward for his own people for allegedly eating the 'apple'. "Some of the examples are horrendous. 200 people died of meningitis in a state, the governor was asked and he said it is God's curse on us for the sin of fornication, which apparently does not happen in America, which is why they don't have meningitis,"[17] the Emir said derisively.

Interesting! What a mind! If America, the headquarters of wholesale fornication or perverted sexual orientations, is exonerated of its guilt by a psycharcinogenic[18] Nigerian Governor, who should be concerned with the gross ineptness of his 7th century-desert-heat-warped-mentality to the welfare of his people who then could have saved his people from the ravages of Meningitis, that just needed only a proactive bold step to procure and distribute VACCINES to them with immediate efficiency?

The rulers (looters) of Nigeria have done a lot of terrible things to this country; the evils they have committed can only be rivalled by those done by the blood-sucking Islamist terrorists, called Boko Haram.

Think about our own Dasukigate scandal, and all the related disreputable 'gates' in your own states and local governments. The elites deliberately crippled the major state institutions, thereby, creating strong individuals but weak institutions. How on earth can a nation of Nigeria's size and magnitude progress without the necessary strong institutions and actionable plans that can cripple *'any big for nothing'* individuals and insane economic saboteurs within its territory? Yet, it has a plethora of strong individuals who use state machinery to assault the sovereignty of the state, rape our collective memory, personalized our commonwealth through 'sellaoutization'[19]in the garment of privatization for better organization.

If the head is bad, the whole of the body will most certainly fall into decay sooner than later. The stagnancy of Nigeria started with the headship and largely remains with them.

Notwithstanding, the largely psycharcinogenic elites, Nigeria still has many amazing people of integrity, very many indeed, women and men of foresight and vision. (Wo)men with a genuine passion for the greatness of Nigeria and liberation of its people from economic, political and psycho-social 'bondages'. Nevertheless, the directionless, aimless, visionless and heartless few who constitute the *leadership gang* have hijacked the machinery of the state for close to 4 decades now, and they have consistently given bad names to good people[20] in order to push them to the margin or edge of our national public life.

They do this so that they (the lootership class) may continue their reign of 'bright' sightlessness, economic terrorism and gross disrespect for the rule of law which kills the growth of the institutions of state. So, they can go on with their deification of *corruption* without being disturbed, challenged or at least tongue-lashed by those genuinely passionate sons and daughters of Nigeria and lovers of its people and sovereignty.

Do We Blame the Senselessly-Religious and Politically Passive Followers?

A bully is only strong to the extent to which his victim is weak. In other words, your level and consistency of resistance determine the boldness of your oppressor to jump at you without any form of hesitation. Unfortunately, the people themselves are the obstacles to those who wish to willingly do and pay everything necessary for the liberation of the state from the grip of these few *animals in human skin,* as Fela Anikulapo-kuti, the late Afro-beat maestro once called them in his *Beast of No Nation* album[21], who are fondling with the testicles of a dying prostrate giant, Nigeria.

Yet, in spite of the giant's excruciating pains their malignant fondling with testicles of our exhausted but not dead giant nation, Nigeria, causes, these heartless few in power never stop saying mockingly about Nigeria to themselves openly and tacitly to us *"testiculos habet et bene pendetes"*[22].

Sadly, however, we (ourselves) have continuously encouraged the 'lootership' (leadership) class to grow stronger in their abominable acts, especially since after the death of ultra-autocratic General Sani Ruthless Abacha (regime) on June 8, 1998 and the eventual return to civil rule, *that is the fourth republic,* on May 29, 1999.

We seem to have always pushed onto the gods/God everything that needs (my and your) our strong reaction –speaking out, condemnation and rejection. All we need is simply making collective call for either the resignation or adjustment of the persons involved in any particular threat to our sovereignty as nation, in any form whatsoever through our subtle but most potent weapon, which is consistent peaceful mass protests in various forms, and by giving more *scathing and critical attention to everyone misbehaving in the position of authority* –public or private, not only the materially rich simpletons in our public life who tend absorb our attention.

We believe prayers to the gods/God will solve everything, while we look on even as our lives are taken from us with next to no resistance. Baba Abami-eda, Fela Anikulapo-kuti , once said in his song that Nigerians are maltreated at will by the ruling elites through their instruments of oppression (uniformed men) because Nigerians give constant excuses for their unjustifiable irrational display of incessant fear in the face of evil by those vagabonds in power:

My people self dey fear too much

We fear for the thing we no see

We fear for the air around us

We fear to fight for freedom

We fear to fight for liberty

We fear to fight for justice

We fear to fight for happiness

We always get reason to fear…"[23] Fela sang. The gods, if they exist in reality, may be there listening to us but they have lost their appetites for terminating their 'perpetual leave' in order to help men and women who have become slaves of their own inactions and senseless submissiveness.

I remember vividly now, how, as a young (teenage) boy in 1993 between July to September, I was almost shot dead at Poly Junction, Ibadan, Oyo state, Nigeria by one of the zombie warlike-soldiers putting down the protests that had erupted as a result of the cancellation of the June 12 presidential election.

The election had been won by MKO Abiola of the Social Democratic Party SDP; and the nation had erupted in massive protests in swift reaction to the senseless act of cancellation by self-styled President of Nigeria, Maradona General Ibrahim Badamosi Babangida, whose regime had been criminally ruining the country for eight uninterrupted years.

I sneaked out to join the protests, and enjoy some protest songs (like Hee…eey una go kill us tire! Hey! Heeey… una kill us, hey hey hey una go kill us tire…). I, at the same time, observed how the adults were fearlessly leading us on Sango end of old Oyo road Ibadan, in response to courageous prodemocracy leaders who didn't expect any gods/God to do our part of the bargain for us.

That experience has made me more defiant of anything oppression-like, no matter how subtle it may be or where it is practised, and so shall it be till my death, amen.

Wait a minute, were the gods dead then? May be, but the real God was in Nigeria and he always will be. But back then we had more of rational prodemocracy leaders, toughened by harsh realities of years of military criminal incursion into politics of governance and the declining wealth and power of the state on one hand, and the inexplicably humongous increase in wealth and reckless (abuse of) powers of certain individuals on the other hand. Had that continued unchallenged, those weakening the state institutions may have felt invincible.

But Nigeria was then Nigeria, not Burundi or North Korea republic or family Kingdom Saudi Arabia, so prodemocracy activists mobilized the nation to resist and it resisted the continuous weakening and crippling of institutions of the state.

Resistance may not *always* get the result you want but it, nevertheless, passes across the message you want: "though you are in charge but don't take me for a fool".

Our religiosity is not as real as it used to be. It lacks depth and it is a psychological protective gear borne out of the desire to run away from the battle lines of reality that tugs at the edge of our politico-economic cloths hourly, as our wealthy nation keeps nose diving economically while a bunch of new tyrants across the 36 states of the federations soar high in opulence. They fly on the wings of our collective wealth at the expense of this nation's development as a whole, that's the simplest of truths!

If the water of illusions with which we (the followers) bathe has NOT been the false expectation of the invasion of Nigeria by some imaginary spineless gods and their gutless, poorly equipped and inexperienced divine armies, who in order to liberate us, installed leaders (looters), may be the damages done and being done to this country by the lootership (leadership?) class might not have reached the level it is currently.

Sadly, however, many of us Nigerians have combined two dangerously destructive substances in our approach to issues affecting the nation namely:

callously-empty religiosity and; culpable political-illiteracy with apathy-and-passivity.

These two elements have consistently blown away the general populace from the front line of resistance to economic oppression by those who rule and 'enslave' us. Consequently, creating easy and unhindered ride to accursed victory for these leaders, who then misrule, mismanage and misdirect the cruise ship of Nigeria, which has now hit a huge rock in the middle of the ocean of atrocities – economic and socio-political.

This collision has made the ship to be stagnant and, this massive and specially built cruise ship[24] named Nigeria is dangerously leaking on the Northeastern flank. The fuel is gushing out in its Niger-delta-coated fuel tank (i.e. Southern flank of the cruise ship) and also some particles are not allowing the remaining gas to flow properly into the engine of the ship.

On the Eastern flank of the ship, however, the occupants are complaining of being neglected by the welfare master of the ship, and even the western flank where the *engine room* is located needs attention of experts because part of the engine is malfunctioning seriously.

And finally, there are gaping holes on both the Northwestern and North central flanks. With the look of things, it seems certain this ship might be lost if those responsible for quick and permanent fixes don't do their jobs promptly and correctly.

Now, you blame whomever it may concern.

God of political prayer in Nigeria, like in many other liberated collective-minds of the world, is dead, and never to rise again! People can only be fools if they choose to be. We or rather I choose not to be, though many of my compatriots have chosen to be fools, and so fools they must be!

Chapter 8

GOD OF POLITICAL PRAYER IS DEAD!

I say it boldly here, without any fear of contradiction, that God of political prayer in Nigeria, like in many other liberated collective-minds[1] of the world, is dead, and never to rise again! People can only be fools if they choose to be, we or rather I choose not to be, though many of my compatriots have chosen to be fools, and so fools they must be!

Although the concept of a dying and rising God/god is not new to orthodox Christians (and perhaps to some other unknown religious believers) since they strongly believe that Jesus Christ is God (the second Person of the Blessed Trinity). That, however, is not my headache here and I am sure, you, the reader, are not interested in that too, at least not here. Yet, to the majority of non-Christian religionists, I mean theists, that is, believers in God/gods of religion who intervene in their affairs, a dying God/god is either inconceivable or not a popular concept!

Anyway, your religious (or non-religious) beliefs, notwithstanding, I know and say again without mincing words that god of political prayer is dead! He dies the very moment he was conceived and projected by his creators -political strategists of the *ruining (ruling) elites* in Nigeria.

The political god of prayer is conceived to deceive. However, deception or falsehood is finite and bound to die by its very nature but the truth is eternal and anything under its shadow is universal and supreme. Therefore, god of political prayer is merely a conceptual being that lives to die in the very factory that produces him – the corruption infested minds of our leaders.

Our elevated and politically bankrolled imams, alfas, pastors, reverends, prophets, evangelists and other religious slaves of titles; religious wealth hunters and juicy-privilege-seekers in the guise of being men of God[2] –actually men of goodies- may continually swarm the seemingly religious services organized by government's agents and their affiliates to pray to a dead or altogether non-existent god(s) of political gimmicks, for all I care, that is a futile effort lacking any spiritual merits. Except, of course, if the divinity being petitioned is an irresponsible being lacking a moral sense of judgment and intellectual capability to objectively analyze the intentions of the people gathered before him, their 'gatherers' and the aims of both colleges of fools!

In fact I have lost count of how many times many hopelessly and irrepressibly underperforming public office holders, especially presidents and governors, senators and local government chairmen go around their religious congregations or groups, under different guises, to have their clerics pray for them in order to perform the very functions for which they are lavishly paid to do as office holders. Fat salaries, abundant allowances, unrivalled right and privileges with little responsibilities are poured on their laps. Yet, their brains refuse to assimilate the message beneath all those largesse from our commonwealth. That message is simple: *"be comfortable in order to manage the state affairs properly for the greatest good of (all/or) the largest majority"*.

But what do we get in return? Failure and gross mismanagement of our commonwealth! And at the end of the day, they will tell the hungry and those poverty-tormented Nigerians to 'fast and pray' for them so that they can do their duties. Then, empty prophecies of something good flow from different convention grounds across the nation to further weaken the already weakened capacities of many Nigerians to challenge the insanely ruinous elites.

Those who honestly but naively fast for them, break their fasting with garri-egba and kulikuli (groundnut cake). Those being fasted for, however, start and end their fasting with milk and honey and a little chicken barbecue feast.

Why should I fast for them? Fast fire! The naivety of the spiritual and political realms is not my luxury. But how many times have those public officials concretely shared their allowances with the poor or real people of no political worth, as they say?

One thing we must get straight is, God is never the one they, the political prayer warriors, pray to because they know that even though he is patient and loving yet he is also *just* and *exacting*. Thus, he would rather stay always with those oppressed, even if is only to console them, instead of enhancing the reign of oppression of the tyrants.

Although theologically speaking, the real God cannot be straight-jacketed, in his eternal wisdom or mysterious ways; he might answer hypocritical prayers in his own way. If, for instance, he sees it (the hypocritical petition) as leading eventually to a greater good that leads to other humanly unforeseen favourable circumstances ahead. Nevertheless, we should not be deceived; he does not listen to hypocritical prayers. That is not his preoccupation because he is not like our national dead political gods.

I guess, for instance, he listened to prayers of Bishop Oyedepo, Pastor Oritsejafor and the band of 'goodie-goodie' pastors and imams that prayed for the re-election of our dear prodigal President Goodluck Jonathan because he lost his reelection bid for the good of Nigeria at that point in time (in 2015). So, their honest prayers, if they are worth being called prayers, were inversely answered by an intelligent God, though he was not the object of their prayers.

Didn't Pastor E.A. Adeboye pray, too? Yes, of course, he did but he had a co-religionist (Pastor-Professor Yemi Osinbajo, a minister in his church) in the race as a vice-presidential candidate which other 'goodie-goodie' clerics mentioned above didn't have. So, his prayer may have different target. I am sure you can 'count your teeth with your tongue'. It is funny, it is sour but it is the stack reality.

Of course, Buhari won the presidential election and Pastor-professor Osinbajo became his vice-president, but it is not as though Buhari's revolutionary walk to Aso-Rock will solve Nigeria's myriad of problems, no it won't. If care is not taken he might end up creating more wahala (disasters) than he solves. His electoral victory, nevertheless, did two very simple things:

i. Ended the monstrously ruinous 16 years of PDP 'overflowing' wastages, and told PDP and its associates 'do it right next time; steal less and work harder'.
ii. It announced this: 'if APC or any government goes down the same path (of looting more and working less) in the future, its' fate could be worse than PDP 2015 electoral misfortunes'.

The point I am making is this, political prayer warriors simply pray to themselves in order to deceive us; they feed on our religious emotions, and those are a powerful flood of human emotions. God has always been with us all, notwithstanding, our political prayers. The problem, however, is that we are not always with him. Funny enough these deceit-maestros are the ones people ignorantly or unthinkingly accept as leaders and the drivers of the beautiful and exceptional 'automobile' called Nigeria.

Unfortunately, some of those who have everything it takes to lead us out of the woods of leadership bankruptcy and economic failure as a nation never had the opportunity to access the driver seat, because as much as they try they are either obstructed by those who profit from the woes of Nigeria or those who have no business being in the driver's seat of Nigeria.

These incapable crowd called moneyticians, occupy public offices with their professional qualification in *incompetence in state administration* and ineffective management of resources; they operate with military precision in corruption and embezzlement and; their mechanical obedience to veiled ethnoreligious pedestrianism is unrivalled.

Ours is a sorry, sad and pathetic society where honourable clowns are the respected chairmen of councils of renowned professors! A society where nonentities dictate the directions for a state populated with honest multidimensional geniuses!

Thus, when these polithiefians realize that the citizens are grumbling or see for themselves that they have veered of the road off slow retrogressive-progression to the jungle of aggressive-regression, they look for an opportunity to shroud the obvious in the mystery of the divine, by injecting the misery-ravaged populace with the *powerful opium known as god-talk or religionism.*

This they do by organizing hyped political prayer services in selected mosques and churches across the nation or states of interest. Super 'goodie-goodie' pastors, reverends, imams, alfas and other legendary privilege-seeking religious simpletons are enlisted for such political prayer sessions; cut-and-sew to fit the naked religious bodies of our brothers and sisters with average religious intelligence.

Government and their partners' radio and television stations air programmes that are tactically and clinically filled with their psycharcinogenic (poisonous-mentality/evil-minded) god-talks and sweet analgesic talk on ceaseless prayers for Nigeria and its' unfortunate looters-in-the-driver's seat called leaders.

One of such prayer jamborees that readily comes to mind now was a group of women that claimed to pray for Oyo state and Nigeria at Remembrance Arcade, Agodi, Ibadan. They were shown live on state-owned television, BCOS, every other Saturday. The wife of the state governor, Mrs Florence Ajimobi, was a regular participant. Once the service was over handouts/takeaways were given to most of the women-participants.

Where did they get the money to fund such jamboree? Was it from the coordinating madam-pastor-prophet's pocket or the office of the first lady?

It is not uncommon for our leaders to have special Jumaat services held on Fridays in major mosques and national mosque; while Sunday services are held in some popular churches, and our museum-like National Christian Centre, Abuja. They are experts at what they do; they induce us with religion and its analgesic through its psycho-emotional sleep-inducing effects. Consequently, we become gullible millions, temporarily forgetting the originators and *nourishers* of our woes – our leaders.

Thus, we bend our knees to our overburdened 'divine' for the good of those who engineer our agonies. Hence, our burdens are not ours alone anymore; it is now shifted to religion or its gods/God for the time being, so it works! Wow!

These guys are amazing magicians and I love their logic because it's stupid.

This approach works like magic on the minds of the poverty enslaved section of the populace! That is why you will hear people saying that *'we must just pray that God should help us…', 'only God can save this country, there nothing anyone can do….'* If you doubt this fact, then survey the opinion (polls) on the internet, listen to radio phone-in programmes and watch TV that does same.

If you are not convinced by what you hear on both media, then turn to your immediate family members and survey their opinions and you will be blown away immediately by the result.

If you will still not trust what you get from your family survey, then please yourself by hitting the streets, gathering opinions and objectively analyzing what you get and the truth will softly kiss your cheek and say: "what you get on the street is what is real."

One thing is clear, politically motivated prayer sessions and religious services are not to appeal to the divine for intervention and mercy, rather they are intended to cajole us –gullible or not- into believing that it is the devil that has to be blamed for their irredeemable ineptitude in doing their work and cancerous corruption.

Oh, you poor devil! Even the devil himself is troubled by their heartless and callous plundering of the national treasury and 'personalization' our commonwealth.

Now, the act of government involvement in organizing prayer services, when ineptitude or greed is ruining the nation, is clearly a smart political tactic. It, no doubt, helps reduce the genuine demands and expectations of the bored populace from a government that is suffering from administrative, managerial and economic impotence, which is likely to degenerate into developmental paralysis if delayed for too long.

These politicians (like their counter-parts across the world),I think, are simply playing out the ideas in their unholy Machiavellian principles as contained in their damned scripture (i.e. the satirical PAGovPat 3:1-2),which says: *"create an illusory aggressive demon from either a person, a nation, an element or the combination of the three entities which the people naturally dislike, suspect to be dangerous or know virtually nothing about*[1]*, and make it a diversion for your heinous crimes by repeatedly and methodically shifting their attention on to their/its' unreal but seemingly threatening activities*[2]. This allows the politicians to have people fear more of an illusory or less threatening enemy than their own politicians who directly threaten their economic existence and socio-political happiness[3].

Thus, our politicians seem *to,* pscharcinogenically and deceptively, reason thus: *'after all the citizens now (deceived to believe they) know who is causing the problems, the devil* [3]*, and so he, not us (the politicians), is to be cast out of the government, and only god can do it* [4] (satirical PAGovPat 3:3-4). Then, they apparently laugh at every moment they deceive themselves and trick our minds this way.

Sadly, however, when you tell yourself too many efficient lies for too long, you start believing them as a fundamental truth, just as they believe their own lies now! So it's the duty of the god(s) to do the never-to-be-done exorcism on the government, thereby making him the object of people's petition instead of the politicians being the object of their *vehement resistance and collective condemnation.*

Wow! What a nice but sick logic! Since the divine is illogically claimed to be responsible for the 'directionlessness' of the ignorant crowd (of politicians) steering the affairs of this nation, and since god is far away up there in his garden or on his holidays above the cloudy skies of the Nigerian political kitchen, therefore, the only way to reach him is to dubiously pray and beg the apparently jobless divine being to come and help us.

Meanwhile, the politicians themselves do not believe he exists in reality. Of course, they know that such jobless being exists only in the thoughts of those (elites) who invented them and those (citizens) who believe the deranged inventors' tricks.

If today our polithiefians and economic-terrorists are sure of any intervention from any real powerful 'divine being', I mean practically more powerful than their government, they will never encourage anyone to pray for its intervention, not even the kings of fools among them will seek his intervention; otherwise they will have their reign of callousness brought to a disastrous end, an end which they dread.

They are economic-vampires sucking financial blood of the nation, and their teeth are the offices they hold. Take away these offices, they will die; and that's why these people will do anything to maintain the supply of financial-blood. You may ask our dear Professor Jerry Gana, Olabode George, Senator Godswill Akpabio and the company of other pathetic politicians who suffer from the infamous and deadly *psychotic power-glue syndrome*[4], and the fact will jump at you.

Consequently, polithiefians and their cohorts tacitly encourage home-grown empty religiosity and superficial spirituality spiced with doses of ethnicism in order to distract the masses and avert, possibly, embarrassing uprising, nationwide protests, mass disobedience and resistance to their insensitive domination.

The level of self-consciousness of Nigerians is at its confusing lowest it was not even like this under the tyrant General Sani Abacha regime. Now, fantastic and weird religiosity has increased and our self-assertiveness and self-consciousness as people have either reduced or vanished altogether. That is significantly due to the systematic effort of the politicians, economic terrorists and other behind-the-scene-but-prominent-collaborators such as the so-called '3rd generation' clerics across the religious spectrum.

In any case, the god of the political prayer services they organize every now and then does not exist, and if anyone claims he exists then I say he exists as a mental resident of those politicians, religionomists and other political opportunists.

He exists in the mind of those who aggressively promote the diversionary and insulting policy of *'a more ill-religious nation, a less thinking people'*[1] (PAGovPat 4:1). Other than that, he is not a being with any rationally justifiable independent existence.

I am not an economic expert but my researches tell me that in every modern functional state, there are two major economic sectors: the real sector (i.e. manufacturing/production) and the commerce sector (i.e. buying and selling, consumption of goods and offering of services. The manufacturing sector, however, is the most important of the sectors imaginable in any modern economy...

Chapter 9

THE ALLIANCE BETWEEN RELIGIONOMICS AND THE NIGERIAN POLITICS

I am not an economic expert, and I do not claim to be one, but I know there are a bunch of theories on economic sectors out there; such as the three-sector theory and the (somewhat now emerging) five-sector theory, and a host of others that do not truly provoke my interest right now.

Yet, as a trained mind, my researches tell me that in every modern functional nation-state, there are two major umbrella economic sectors: the real sector (i.e. manufacturing/production/extracting sector) and the commerce sector (i.e. buying and selling/consumption of goods and services). The manufacturing sector, however, is the most important of all the sectors imaginable in any modern economy.

Therefore, responsible and prudent ruling class makes sure that the real sector of the economy is systematically planned, developed and jealously protected, so that in the long run the poverty level of the populace is reduced, thereby minimizing debilitating effects of poverty on human mind.

On the contrary, in Nigeria, a fairly modern and stable state but not so structurally functional as it deserves, the politicians have continuously reinforced an ephemeral economic subsector -superficial religiosity- that produces more men and women of below-average religious intelligence. This act gives them more control over the lives of these people directly and indirectly through their so-called men of (goodie-goodie) god; I mean the traders of religion or religion's businessmen[1] (and women).

The Nigeria's deceptive religious environment has probably bred more holy hell's birds than the devil's oven expects from a single human territory in the last 20 years.

Now, every fool is a pastor or general overseer and every idiot is an imam or sheik. Imagine, as though people await their arrival (of marketers of religion), their emergence on the scene of religion is greeted with laughter and open-arms by a significant mass of people in any particular space they surface. Therefore, on the part of the majority of the people, there is little or no intellectual examination or *resistance*[2] to these usurpers of true religious space.

Having won followers and carved out territories for themselves in the minds of many, they start 'seeing voices and hearing visions'[3]. These dramas endear them to the 'spiritually' blind, deaf and dumb political office holders, and to innumerable religious *nincompoops*. These marketers have their interests, which are money, fame and power. And the politicians do have their interests as well, which include, but not limited to, continuous control of the machinery of the state at the expense of the common good. Therefore, there is a meeting point; the prostitute meets the thief, and the blend is now perfect!

As a result, our politicians fund these religion marketers in cash and kind, in other words, donating to their religious houses, granting them outrageous privileges and tacitly supporting their interests with state powers[4]. While the marketers of religion (or religionomists) in turn, encourage their followers to pray ceaselessly for the good of the politicians concerned, and often subtly praise them in the public for every feat they achieve in failure.

In addition, they declare their support for them and manipulate their followers, clients, congregations or customers to do the same because it is a holy thing to do. In fact, some go to the extreme by publicly proclaiming that certain politicians in question are divinely elected or anointed to run for office(s).

This has been a very efficient and potent socio-religious phenomenon in Nigeria. Of course, I am not insinuating it is an exclusively Nigerian disease, no, but my interest here and now is in Nigeria, so I talk about Nigeria as I know it. Politics in Nigeria is a multibillion naira industry, and religion-marketing is also a strong multibillion naira industry as well with its ever-expanding shrouded capital base. Both Religionomics[5] and politics in Nigeria are interested in powers, no matter how you see it that is the primary drive or the governing propensity of both 'sciences of manipulation' or arts of deception.

While Religionomists (religion marketers) are interested in achieving that through the instrumentality of the distorted religion, the politicians rely on lots of sophistries, alliances, collaborations and manipulations to achieve their aim.

Religionomics has actually eaten so deep into the fabrics of this society that most politicians now see it as the most viable alternative to brute force and a reliable partner in evil of short-changing the masses. So, their calculation is 'let us feed this monstrous phenomenon (Religionomics) very well with what it eats: title, wealth, privileges and fame, and it will enslave the minds of millions to further our political manipulations'.

The alliance between politics and religionomics is systematic, well-oiled and potent. It may or may not be a conscious effort, I don't know and I don't care, all I know is, it exists; because we are living with it. Without yielding to sentimentality, you can imagine with what immense prejudice these people interact with the citizenry on 'economic tsunami' wrecking our lives apart.

Of course, their prejudice is a natural result of such union between these two groups whose desires are almost the same in degree, intensity and consistency: domination, possession and control, simple. This alliance grows every day and more marketers of religion are flexing their muscles, covering more spaces and aligning themselves to useful political forces. Consequently, what is emerging in Nigeria's socio-political and psycho-religious spheres is a configuration that is similar to what the medieval (6th to 15th century Europe) period was made up of; although, there is a huge difference in style, fashion, society and century.

This impressive drama of absurdity has been unfolding or still being played out by the actors themselves in this our beloved Nigeria. Therefore, I am not writing in the manner of a story crafted from an idea or an idea reformulated as a fact, but rather as a reality *put together as a reflection,* so that we look beneath the surface of the current religio-political structures and challenge our current understanding of both the public of holders and their collaborators.

This event itself, a fact that is in public domain, is my object of reflection here and we should do the understanding together for our common good.

My fear, however, is that if the trend continues, Nigeria as a nation will continue to produce politically confused people. In other words, people who cannot make any reasonable decryption of many of the shrewdly encrypted political gimmicks being played out at a particular point in time by the politicians and the marketers of religion. The after effect of this is more wretchedness and smoother backwardness[6] for our religiously disposable 'materials' of religionomists, and the 'territory' of the politicians –that is the people and the country.

I have heard, over and over again, the saying that (Nigerian) politics is a dirty game and is too dirty for upright men! Well, irrespective of the validity or absurdity of this saying, it is a fundamental universal view that politicians are cunning, dishonest and manipulative…

Chapter 10

POLITICS IS TOO DIRTY FOR UPRIGHT MEN

The world without is a reflection of the world within[1]. What we often complain about are merely the effects of a cause -our thought. I have heard, over and over again, the saying that (Nigerian) politics is a dirty game and it is too dirty for upright men! Well, irrespective of the validity or absurdity of this saying, it is a fundamental universal view that politicians are cunning, dishonest and manipulative; from the Peoples Republic of China to the United States and from the Russian Federation to the United Kingdom, and from Rome to Tehran the story is the same. However, their cunningness varies from nation to nation depending on the stability and strength of state institutions. I mean the capacity of the state 'guard-dogs' to bite the erring politicians where it hurts more if they trample on its laws and statutes, policies and integrity.

But now, back to Nigeria, I have a question; who are the upright men and what makes politics too dirty for them?

If the so-called upright men do not join politics when they have the capacity to, whom do they expect to fill the void of righteousness caused by their 'upright absence': angels or spirit or demons? Who?

I have come to realize that no politics, anywhere in the world, is dirtier than the society in which it is practised[2]. Consequently, everyone who claims that politics is dirty in Nigeria is a part of the society that produces that dirty politics and, therefore, they are by-products of the same society that generates heaps of the so-called dirty game, namely politics.

If they, those who claim to be upright, are not stained with the filth generated by the same society that produces the so-called dirty politics, then it means that their uprightness, if it is not a farce, should be able to gradually wash or half-clean the filthy cloth of Nigeria's politics.

The point here is that their uprightness or (their) 'moral and political detergent' should have some stain removing effects on our politics, especially from the most sensitive areas of the political cloth, such as the armpits (looting) and collar (cronyism), and make it as sparkling as humanly possible, with the hope that whatever principle or force or agent is responsible for their preservation (of the upright men) will come to party again in this venture of higher value of developmental politics for the common good of all.

Besides, if it is not a smokescreen, their uprightness should be able to emit powerful rays of light[3] that dispel the thick darkness in which our politics (and the society that gives birth to it and nurses it) fumbles about in such nauseating multi-dimensional darkness for direction.

Darkness, you should know, signifies retrogression, backwardness, underdevelopment and one-thousand-and-one other things that represent only: Immobility, Lifelessness, Decay or Stagnation. Almost nothing grows in the dark except regressive and cunning creatures. Light, on the other hand, signifies life, rejuvenation, progress, mobility and growth. And, in its various forms, light is the most essential element for sparking creative development.

It follows, logically, therefore, that if the politics in Nigeria is dirty it means the society is somewhat in darkness and its darkness is somehow a reflection of the thought pattern of a large chunk of both the leaders and the people of such society in which it is found. Consequent upon this, if it continues without being checked by a higher value (light of uprightness), then, sooner than later nothing will grow or progress again within its boundaries as it should be and when it should. The reason is that the strength of the darkness will increase and one day it will consume or cripple or expelled the so-called upright men from its area of dominance, in this case, Nigeria.

As the saying goes, *what it takes evil (men) to cancerously fester is for good (men) to reflexively watch without doing anything.* For example, as big as the main bow of Liberty Stadium (now Obafemi Awolowo stadium) in Ibadan is, in the darkest of nights and the most starless and moonless of night skies, when absolute darkness reigns absolutely, if a candle stick is lit and put on small matchbox in the centre circle of the pitch of that gigantic edifice, everyone who comes into that arena at that point in time, or has been sitting in that darkness infested arena before that candle is lit, will see it.

If that person does not have sight impairment he will not only see it from far within the main bowl, he will feel a sense of liberation from the mental laceration the prevailing absolute darkness has been inflicting on him. If he decided to move from his current position in the main bowl, he can calculate his direction by that tiny tongue of flame on the light-emitting candle in the heart of the enormous darkness in which he is enveloped. Think about that and gain wisdom.

For this reason, therefore, we need to start a psycho-social restructuring which will emit *therapeutic process of collective transformation* of our socio-political 'atmospheres'. There must, however, be a rallying point or unifying agents for or in this whole process. Hence, it is necessary and indispensible to have agents of genuine transformation that will stimulate this process of psycho-social change and mental purification. This purification of our psycho-social and mental states will lead, eventually, to that humanly achievable level of cleaner science of social cohesion, organization and governance for better living which we call 'sane politics'.

With this in mind, the politically capable upright men and women should come out of their comfort zones, and collaborate with those men and women already fighting day and night for the liberation of Nigeria and its people from the domination of our homegrown imperialists and their international collaborators. In that way, they become the rallying point for the much needed integrity propelled change of (political) batons and (government) sprinters in this seemingly endless relay race of shame.

So that once again the race becomes a race of fame spiced with genuinely superior logical ideas for elevation of the masses and the green white green. This will allow our best qualified sprinters possible to win the race for us all, through us all and by us all, most of the time.

As Nigerians of goodwill with fervent love of your fatherland, it is part of your patriotic obligations to serve Nigeria with all your strength by upholding its honour and glory.

But what honour will be left if Nigeria is governed perpetually by men and women of the underworlds in the *Turban-Roman collar*[4] or Khaki-Agbada[5] raised from among us by our own indifference or mental and moral laxity?

Which glory will be left to defend if these so-called evil men, who have their eyes on their heels, uproot all men of goodwill from the land?

Which glory will be left when their actions make it impossible for many (of us) Nigerians to see anything good in their own sacred home land anymore except in foreign lands where they are treated like modern slaves?

Do you people expect all of us to leave the sweetness of the land that *loves* our very breath for a land we live in cultural limbo, economic uncertainty and identity flux before you start thinking?

Will all of you, the so-called righteous men, have peace in this land by then? Or are you waiting till everything that can bring you down even to six-feet beneath the surface of the earth is deployed by these 'pigs' who find their joy in the current muddy, mucky and filthy lake of the corridors of power?

What is the essence of the righteousness that cannot dispel the gloom of reigning moral evil and socio-political atrocities and economic darkness?

If Nigerian politics is truly dirty, as many of you claim, then, be the bleach! Otherwise shut up, because it will never get an inch cleaner if upright men sit in their houses and nag in the corner of their rooms day and night.

Tell me, dear righteous men and women, where in the history of the world has anyone improved his life by simply nagging and instinctively doing nothing? Are you a man of principles but not wealthy? Step out, Nigerians need your principles. We need your leadership, like we used to have during the murderous the Abacha regime, no matter how insignificantly minute it might be in the ocean of the unprincipled lot swarming our public life nowadays.

Or you are wealthy but do not have strong political interest or principles yet you want to finance those who have what you lack without expecting profits, honestly? Then, you are a good ingredient for this social change, this psychological transformation and socio-political revolution. Start emitting your light of integrity in your street, ward, district, local government area, state etc., and the change will start emerging and encircle the entire nation someday, one day, very soon.

The point is, the change begins with the transformation of your mental attitude. If you do not start the process for collective reorientation by sincerely acknowledging that a dirty public life of a state will not so much change if men of unbending sincerity (like you) do not start the dry-cleaning process in their own little terrains; that is, their minds and immediate environments.

Having said that much above, I will like to say clearly that that we have had in the past and even at present men of unquestionable moral strength. Men who have shown us in terms of their practical daily living, that no matter how dirty or dark or gloomy our public life (politics and related spheres) might be, their uprightness can reduce its areas of influence, even if it is an inch, by emitting their own light in their own sphere of influence, not necessarily by ballot box or office-seeking politics but in whatever sphere they can initiate the much needed transformation.

There were and there are still several examples of these men, and they include: late Chief Bola Ige, Gani Fawehimi, Pa Alfred Rilwan, Aminu Kano , Dele Giwa, Barrister Femi Falana, Pastor Tunde Bakare, Edmund Obilo and many wonderful others.

In addition, we should note that sometimes when you hear people complain about the filthy state of politics when they have capacity to do something for the society and won't do it but nag, especially in Nigeria, they do it in order to cover their own infirmities or frightful shadows.

Politics is dirty, but is it dirtier than any major business enterprise anywhere in the world? To be more specific, politics is an art and a 'scientific game' of bargaining, no game is dirtier than the players. Every game has its point of accidents, that's why there are rules to reduce those accidents, or 'dirtinesses' if you like, because without the players a game is merely a mental construct with no realistic existence.

So, like any other fields of social interactions, politics' dirtiness is dependent on the participants - righteous, religionomists, moneyticians, politicians, economic-terrorists and the voters (me, you and others). Wait a minute, don't business men without basic ethical standards find joy in ripping consumers off anywhere in the world, even in the so called first crazy world? Is that dirty or clean? Oh, it's clean because it not party politics? You are ignoramus!

What we often hear from the majority of the so-called upright but incapable men whenever they condemn politics is: "I cannot join politics....because it's too dirty". Interesting, isn't it? Yet, you run businesses where you bargain with the demons and angels daily. Hold on a second, my question to you is, what do you intend to say; I 'cannot join' or 'will not join'? Because, technically, *cannot join* and *will not join* are never the same things.

Analyzing these two phrases in the context of actual thought patterns reveals something. If they are really men of firm minds, men given to accurate expression of their thoughts and their intentions they should know that, "I cannot join...because its dirty" suggests that many of them actually are scared of something, and that *might be* the possibility that their real colour behind the scenes[6] might be exposed. Or they are just incapable, incompetent and unqualified to lead, their so called uprightness, notwithstanding.

Why would any reasonable person keeps condemning a system that determines your very peace and progress within its territory as dirty, and you won't push people forward by words or action to attempt the needed change for the improvement of the system and society? Why?

I don't get it, it makes little sense. Anyway, on the other hand, "I will not join because.... I don't have the interest", technically speaking, means I *have or may have the* capacity or cleaner closet to be a part of the political process of this country for greater good and I am mentally, emotionally and socially stable to be a leader of my people (Nigerians) with no skeleton in my wardrobe, but I will not join the process for any reason. Why? Because it's not my area of interest its dirtiness or cleanliness, notwithstanding.

Wow, so in much little. I think that (the latter) makes a little sense more than the former, yet both lack the moral authority to condemn the system without, at least, psychologically pushing human elements forwards for the needed change.

It's a kind of cursing the darkness without lighting the candle in your hand by reaching out for a match stick in the matchbox. That's why Matthew 5:14-16 says a reasonable person will not just curse the darkness when he has capacities to light up the world around him. So, where is your righteousness?

In any case, you don't have to have your name on the ballot paper to be part of the process, you can be a financier or adviser or behind-the-scene strategist of an honest and principled young (wo)man in your ward or local government area; I mean just do something good to energize the needed change. Even if you are a cleric, learn from honest ones around you like Pastor Bakare, and use part of your homilies/sermons for educating your flocks on genuine participation in the transformation of the political process and not just preach tithing all your life.

Well, we may never know the actual state of your mental capability or incapability, but what is certain in the above arguments is that the flimsy argument that Nigerian politics is too dirty for (the) good, upright or principled men is a beautiful sophistry or at best an irrelevant fallacy.

If those who can and should contribute to the development and sustenance of a cleaner public life or less dirty national politics refuse to join, or are too cowardly to step out for a change, in spite of the fact that things are deteriorating every day, politically and economically, then, the politics will get dirtier, filthier and murkier to the extent that the stench coming from the decaying system will choke Nigerians in their millions; and one way or the other you, too, Mr. and Mrs. Capable but cowardly upright man and woman, will be affected. Aren't you affected already?

If men and women of firm moral discipline will not participate in politics because they see it as a dirty game, like I have always said, then there will be an absence of their much needed inspiring presence which is required to make sense out of our politics of prevailing nonsense.

If men and women of stable integrity abstain from the current politics of common nonsense, a political culture which humiliates the dreams of our founding fathers, then the empty space invented by your inactivity, immobility, indolence, lethargy, idleness or apathy will be occupied by the filth producing political bacteria. It is no rocket science, nature detests vacuum.

These human bacteria will produce volumes upon volumes of bad political smell (dirtier politics) and more organized-cell structure (party) that is ruthless, they will participate in it (politics) alone, and these bacteria will generate more crippling diseases (evil policies) for us all (you and me).

In other words, the dirty politics will get dirtier, dirtier people will run it; only dirtier people will vie for offices. Then you and your household will ratify their employment (whether you vote or not: your inaction or action has meaning). On assumption of office, dirtier people will enact dirtier laws and oppressive policies for your generation and generations to come; they will make your offspring lick their boots and that of their offspring, just as you see them do all around you.

These dirtier people will entertain dirtiest economic plans that devalue the naira, discourage exportation, and encourage massive importation, and your children will trek to the collective West or other places they are not accepted looking greener pasture while the greenest pasture is consumed by our own leaders-turned-grasshoppers (the so called dirty people) at home.

These dirtier people will cripple national institutions and facilities that have extreme negative economic implications on the masses, such as our refineries, national (electricity) power grid etc. The list of the dirty things these filthy-minded people can generate when not checked by hygiene-minded (the upright) people, is endless.

If your uprightness is not a farce or a pretense, then, you should know that you can write your name eternally in bronze for doing nothing when you can or write it perpetually in gold by joining forces with other men and women of good will, and work for the reduction of filth in Nigeria politics by acting as hygienic-cum-corrective agent for the filth infested political field.

You don't have to be the 'best' or the 'holiest', there is no such thing in politics. All you need to do is to arm yourself with integrity, honesty, knowledge and unflinching passion for the common good.

....As body without spirit is dead, so is faith without effort (practical action/ works, protests or resistance movements) is dead.

Chapter 11

THE DESTRUCTIVE EFFECT OF GOD-DEYISM

Different phases and dimensions of our lives; religious, social, cultural, academic, political - especially in the corridors of power - have been made bold in evils of various kinds and degrees by the *Goddeyism effects* (there is God effect) on the mentality of many of us, Nigerians.

This unconscious (perhaps, conscious) sickness constantly cripples our potent but latent power to demand purposeful leadership, or at least ask for our right as a people to whom the nation belongs; after all, we are neither North Koreans nor Saudi Arabians.

'Goddeyism'? What do you mean by that? You may ask, and I will tell you, I am not creating the condition I am only naming a festering circumstance that is already here with us. So, I will say, it is our collective attitude of mind that perpetuates strong but sickly emotions of total powerlessness in the face of defeat-able tyranny.

Many of us, in our daily lives across every section of the society, face or experience despotism, domination and/or oppression at various levels from different perpetrators -uniformed men and women, the street fathers and landlords, the rich and connected, religious figures, politicians and their cohorts in power. In spite of these daily realities, we never seem to see any reason take appropriate steps; no matter how little but significant these steps might look.

Instead, we want God to do it for us. As a consequence, God is expected to fight for us or on our behalf at the appropriate time. Hence, the (common) saying in pidgin, *make dem they cheat us, we know say God na the hope wey we get and, he go fight for us one day*[1]. Meaning: let them (people in power) continue to misrule us, God, at the appropriate time, will fight for us and/or deliver us one day.

This psycho-religious orientation, like any other form of self-imposed psychological paralysis, has never helped any person who indulges in it -by design or accident- because it makes him a slave in circumstances he naturally should have been the master.

God has given man powers to challenge and change everything for good or bad -whichever way he wants; those powers are always there in him. Authorities are to be respected not worshipped, honoured not feared, supported for common good only not enslaved by them; and challenged if they transform to ravenous wolves instead of being the loving but firm shepherds. It is, however, a tragedy when 'Goddeyism' has become a way of life for many of the citizens of this nation.

Yes, God-dey (there is God), we or rather I do not, at any rate, have any doubt about that, neither do I doubt His Omnipotence, Omniscience and Omnipresence. No, I doubt none of these divine qualities or, put more properly, essences. And I do not need to be told that God listens to those who call on him from their hearts[2] while doing their proper part of the bargain. As a young man, my personal life experience is a testimony to this fact.

What is, however, false, unreal and religiously irrational is the abdication or rejection of our role in the scheme of things in any given circumstance; and then decide to go through unimaginable but avoidable agonies, tortures, sufferings or pains while waiting for, in most cases, imaginary divine wrath or vengeance to come on those who oppress us. That is nothing but mild madness and an inexplicably repelling mental stench, to calmly put it.

After all, those who oppress their fellow countrymen and women are human beings like those they oppress, but the major difference between them and us is that they use their own will-power, their mental energy to scheme and achieve what they want, when they want and how they want it. They use their energies so well, to the extent that they (the oppressors) use their God-given powers to shrewdly manipulate or buy or altogether steal the God-given but largely dormant inner-powers of other citizens.

They are able to exploit our inner powers (because we are either too lazy to use our them or ignorant of their existence) without our knowledge, through the exploitation of our different religious, ethnic and other primordial currencies-of-emotions[3] on which our lives are run daily, thereby, keeping us in some form voluntary and mild but unreasonable bondage. Yet, we, the oppressed people, are saying there is God, is it not funny? The oppressors themselves, in the heart of their hearts, still firmly or subtly or cunningly or cleverly tilt toward the belief in an unseen but ever-present almighty force that makes things work their way; although, they may not have the right conceptual name for it, or misunderstand the morals of its presence altogether.

Accordingly, this is not the case of thinking there is God out there to intervene and solve the problems associated with our oppression when we should have played our role of active agitations for our rights. Agitations that either make the authorities concerned bend, where the greater good is obvious or break altogether when and where their selfish, myopic, egotistic and mundane self-interest is the medal for the for tyranny and/or oppression being imposed on us.

In my view, it is a case of (if truly we are believers in God's Omnipotence) acknowledging, *understanding and opening*[4] of ourselves to the ever-present abundant graces of God; and peacefully, carefully, consistently and actively demanding for what truly is ours -freedom from every form tyranny, no matter how minute it might be.

We shout all the time 'there is God' when we are confronted with challenges from maladministration and mismanagement, though beneath the surface, we are not as righteous as we claim. But I think, in the context of our expected active participation in our own salvation, this constant noisy call on the divine without the corresponding action will not save the situation.

This mental attitude is a sign of multi-faceted laziness. Actually, we are, if this mental attitude continues, gradually falling into a kind of prison of 'quietism'[5] or 'silentism'[6] (that is, *sidon-look*) that may make us more easily abused, molested and *ruined* by our rulers: religious, socio-cultural, academic, military and paramilitary, economic and political rulers -all of them.

The ruin which, I am sure, is not the aim of God for us but which in the recent history of Nigeria, for the most part, is self-induced and self-sustaining.

Put differently, our outrageously irrational understanding of the powers of the divine government and its ordered relationship[7] with/to the temporal powers, and authorities can only encourage any *mean* or bad-tempered or *power-crazy* person or group of callous persons in control of government and its' apparatus to take the worst advantage of the period of our waiting for divine intervention for vengeance on them, and do with us whatever they want.

Nigeria fought for independence of many African nations and stabilized a host of others. We were active as a nation back then, because we had policymakers and implementers who unconsciously understood Exodus 14:15-16 and 17-18, man's active role and God's active graces or roles. But all that seem to have gone with the winds because we are abdicating our roles now because we are internally sick.

The history of independence of some nations in Africa is not complete without mentioning the roles Nigeria played. Now, it is a shame to hear the same Nigerians (of all people to) speak and pray anxiously for an improvement in our circumstances, yet we are *unwilling to improve our mental-strength and rationally realistic psycho-religious* approach to political and socio-existential issues. I mean issues that need our spontaneous but ordered and determined actions against (and not reactions against) anyone caging or trying to cage our basic human rights and other constitution-guaranteed rights and privileges as the real owners of the Nigerian state.

Consequently, we are bound to pillars of miseries that infuriate and repel even the divine government we claim is in our support. And rather than stir its sympathy and draw its vengeance and retribution on our oppressors, we, apparently, draw its anger on ourselves for our nauseating Goddeyismic attitudes without actions.

Therefore, understanding the appropriate interplay between the divine powers and the temporal powers will help us to know that praying to God does not replace the active tasks expected of us. Although, the divine supersedes the temporal yet the divine does not break its own law needlessly.

We must bear in mind the fact that everything in creation is the product of order (ordered thought) not confusion (confused expectations), thus both in the visible and invisible worlds the preeminent standard guiding the operations in and of those realms is Order/Law, not confusion or disordered expectations.

It follows, therefore, that while the intervention of the divine and the eternally superior government may be rightly anticipated sometimes by men and women of any territory, especially Nigeria; it cannot be taken to be a norm, law or proper part of the divine governance. God is not a lawbreaker! He is the lawmaker and law enforcer! Interventions are, like in any legal entity, exceptions and cannot be taken as part of the standard rule!

We all know, for instance, that anyone who has the aim of making it in life MUST be ready to make great sacrifices (mental, social, emotional, physical and psychic etc) before he can realize his dream because success is a product/result of a process,[8] and a process is a combination of laws, rules or instructions that are expected to be carried out in order to hit a specific target. So how much more will millions of people who are determinedly pragmatic in their approach to life, achieve, if they make necessarily sensible sacrifices?

Accordingly, if truly our Goddeyism is genuinely a reflection of our inner spiritual characters, then we will know for certain that there is a problem with our religion, no matter the title or name it carries. The reason is that a rationally and eternally active God could not have created an inactive and semi-rational or fully-irrational yet instinctive[9] *beings in his own image*. Beings that run away from challenges they are equipped to solve psycho-spiritually, physiologically, mentally, economically and socio-politically. If he did, then there is a huge question mark on his rationality and creativity as an eternal creator-being.

In the end analysis, Nigerians, home and abroad, should know that if what we seek always in any situation that challenges our existence and happiness as a people or collectively -east, west, north and south– is not to use the God-given powers in us, then we are sick beyond descriptions. These powers help us master our challenges and rise against and above (those challenges or) our oppressors and their collaborators in different shades-and-colours, especially those in the pulpits.

It is holy and worthy for us to stand firm in the defence of our God-given rights, and not sit back and look on, expecting God to save us from a situation that is not beyond our response-ability.

If we 'sidon-look' while our rulers-turned-captors grow stronger in evils of various degrees, then our faith in God is dead or never existed and we are the most unfortunate of religionists!

"…Show me this faith of yours without your effort (works/actions), then! And I will by my efforts (works/actions) show you my faith…You believe in the One God – that is credible enough, but even the demons (including politicians, economic-terrorists, religionomists and cohorts) have the same belief, and they tremble with fear. Fool! Would you not like to know that faith without effort (practical actions or works or peaceful but persistent agitation) is useless…As the body without the spirit is dead, so is *faith without effort (practical action/ works, protests or resistance movements, involvement in political process, exposure of fake pastors and imams) is dead*"[10].

...Education is a technique that opens you up to information from different sources, equips you with intellectual sieve or filter to separate necessity from want, prejudice from objectivity, ideal from reality; and in the end make you a better human being with logically sharp and distilling mind, that makes you broad-minded by liberating you from your narrow-mindedness and your little above-animal-level-intelligence.

Chapter 12

'MENTALLY LAZY' BUT MATERIALLY GREEDY GENERATION

All Politicians Are the Same, So Why Worry?

If there is any strong root for the psycho-religious-cum-spiritual, socio-cultural and politico-economic captivity of Nigeria as a nation, I dare say, it is largely because of our descent into intellectual indolence, and rational and/or logical sophistry[1].

Since the intellectual strength is the control unit of other facets of man, once it malfunctions or is dishonest, then, there is a problem on the horizon of such life. Of course, it is not everyone that is involved in this plunge, but a huge and an alarming chunk is guilty of it.

If the majority of the older generations involved are forgiven of their intellectual dishonesty or slothfulness because it favours them, what do we do with 'the younger generations'[2], who are said to be the leaders of tomorrow? I don't get it, which of the 'tomorrows' are we talking of: the uncertain one, the awful and shaky one or the non-existent one?

This is a generation (in Nigeria of today where almost every child starts schooling from pregnancy) that can confidently boast of the experience of early schooling among a huge chunk of its members. That is, from the elementary to the intermediate to the higher education with the acquisition of different pre-graduate, graduate and postgraduate qualifications upon completion of their training, even the most seemingly irrelevant and almost useless qualifications, before its average member turns 28 years[3].

The level of schooling or education available to this generation, which a meaningful or sizeable number of its members have taken and are still taking advantage of, is phenomenal! Every year tens of thousands[4] of students are churned-out by various higher institutions in the country, whether fully baked or half-baked or not baked at all.

Admittedly, this is not peculiar to Nigeria (alone); it affects many other nations across the world too. Since a lot of youths just want to be 'rich' overnight without sweating at all. However, on the pages of this section, I am concerned about the youths of Nigeria only, not those of the world.

We are a generation loaded with talents and qualifications; there are doctorate, masters and first degree holders all over the place, not forgetting diploma (ND&HND) and various classes of certificate holders. Special training facilities that offer mixture of vocational and formal education for school leavers and graduates increase every now and then, which is good, not bad.

However, even with its exposure to schooling or education at age earlier than the generations before it, this generation still exhibits an unacceptable level mental/intellectual lethargy, laziness, slothfulness or sluggishness which has made it, for the most part, terribly and logically empty and superficial and; irritatingly dishonest in its scholarly approach to socio-existential issues that are very conspicuous in today's Nigeria.

Put simply, *it lacks depth when engaged on existential issues* that are thrown up every now and then by the socio-political and ethnoreligious matrices (i.e. prevailing conditions) of its immediate community -Nigeria.

This generation of Nigerians is, in terms of information availability and accessibility, the most privileged of all the generations of Nigerians. This is the generation that is having direct access to information and communication technology[5] and all the available technological gadgets associated with it.

This generation has mighty tons and loads of information all around it and can be made available to it and its members at the press of a button or by just clicking **"Ok or Go!"** Yet, this is almost the least informed of Nigerian generations when it comes to existential and socio-political logic and, I dare say, compared to other generations, the most ignorant of matrix[6] of existential happenings in its immediate environment.

This generation goes about with the most sophisticated gadgets modern technology in all its glory in the field of information and communication technology has to offer, yet this generation is almost always mal-informed[7], dis-informed[8] and in the end analysis, uninformed[9] about the most germane existential issues in its immediate environment, Nigeria.

What we understand education to mean will affect how we approach it and what we ultimately get from it in terms of intellectual sharpness and shrewdness.

There is a general misconception about education in this generation; it is commonly seen as a tool for earning a living. While this may not be totally wrong if and when taken as part of what it is supposed to be, it will be, however, irredeemably wrong if the real underlying principle of what education means is substituted as a whole for this superficial logic of 'for job only'.

In fact, this orientation is (extensively) rampant and almost becoming an incontestable dictator in the psychological template that guides the manners of many students of this generation and their pitiable parents, guardians and sponsors who belong to the older generations that are expected to have deeper thoughts on things but, sadly, who are not so much different from their dangerously sick succeeding generation.

Yet, again I say this is not peculiar to Nigeria; I witnessed the orientation in the US too. When in the situation of critical national conversations, emotions take the place of the simplest logical reasoning even among the university students. But I am concerned about Nigeria because, within the context of our development, ours is distressing.

Education, as I have always told fellow youths if properly acquired, *is a technique that opens you up to information from different tested (and sometimes, untested) sources, equips you with intellectual sieve or filter to separate necessity from want, prejudice from objectivity, and ideal from reality;* and in the end make you a better human being with logically sharp and distilling mind, that makes you broad-minded by liberating you from your narrow-mindedness and your little above-animal-level-intelligence. In other words, it (education) makes you a structured learner, a rational person who can always extract information from the most minute and insignificant phase of life anywhere at any time.

Thus, taking education as a means to an end as opposed to taking it as an end[10] in itself, is the broad and well-paved road to producing (and being a member of) a generation that is mentally shallow, myopic, superficial and ultimately, intellectually lazy and scholarly indolent. A (mere) disaster waiting to happen, if not happening already! Even if all your needs in life are provided for, to be better than the dolphins you need structured knowledge for a fruitful life.

Consequently, a properly educated[11] generation or a generation that claims to be educated cannot but know the fact that human beings are relational beings and, a relationship is naturally a simple but complex social phenomenon. And so, many matrices are at play at various levels of human relationships, but many of these (matrices i.e. surrounding circumstances) are so subtle and almost non-existent such that it seems they have no force, impact or effect on what direction our relationships take. While on the other hand, a handful of other matrices may have prominent effect on (our relationships) them.

Thus, understanding this fact opens the windows of our minds to the ever-rising sun of knowledge which illumines the dreadful night of our conscience and perception thereby forcing servile ignorance to recede from the fertile land of our intelligence to a territory of non-existence.

This generation of ours -though a reflection of its own society- is a shame to its self for not allowing the power of the liberating knowledge acquired to have its foothold in its thought pattern. This is a generation that places 'blind' emphasis on what you possess, not what values you can contribute to the growth of the community. What you have or are[12] as opposed to *whom you are* or your *capacity for growth*[13].

This is a generation that sees 'hard' but meaningfully 'smart' work as the portion of the unwise or people of low intelligence quotient (I.Q.) who do not know their ways. What a generation with little understanding of words and concepts it uses so carelessly!

They complain bitterly about the politicians and our leaders generally, and even some about their parents, not because they would be any better if allowed to lead, but because they want to skip the proper process of growth and live the sort of, supposedly meaningless, life those they complain about are living.

I mean they (the males) want to drive flashy cars with no work, if possible, while still in 100 levels and girls all around them as though they are decoration materials. While the females, on the other hand, want to buy expensive clothes, handbags and other fashionable materials and possessions that are eternal signs of profligacy; and nothing more.

They think reading without having an examination in view is advanced or full-fledged waste of time, listening to unbiased news bulletin is a pastime for the fools, reading newspapers and investigative journals is for those who want to have hypertension, reading autobiographies, biographies and books of realistic, philosophical, existential, mind sharpening, informative and life-transforming contents is a prison -gentlemanly called boredom, which they do not wish to be involved or imprisoned in!

Why does this generation ridicule almost everything that can inject more meaningful life and direction into the minds of its members? I think the answer is simple; it is because it cannot derive immediate financial gains or material gratifications and social-show-offs from such activities. What a decaying or rotten generation is this?

Therefore, it follows necessarily that, *if we* have truly been (educated as we claim and) equipped with the logical filter needed for separating fact from fiction or for knowing the appropriate boundaries between the government propaganda and the reality in any situation that the politicians (moneyticians, religionomists, economic-terrorists) and their collaborators try to confuse us with, by presenting us with the perplexing doses of '*faction*'[14] instead of either an outright fact or plain fiction, because they know that people anywhere in the world are easily confused when facts are shrewdly mixed fictitious pieces and presented as pieces of genuine information, *then we* shall know the truth and this knowledge of the truth shall set us free.

With the humongous data available to this generation daily, should we not have known about the elite psycho-political remote control systems worldwide, which psycharcinogenic leaders use to stay relevant in power for many years?

The elite-gimmick principle runs thus: 'the *fact in the 'faction' draws* the recipient's attention and prompts him to open up himself to the ideas in the message[1], once that is achieved, if the recipient has no intellectual 'antibodies' (i.e. if he doesn't question the official narratives) or has no strong 'intellectual territorial armed forces' (i.e. he doesn't check to see if there are necessary or unnecessary connections in an information they present to him), then *the fictitious elements in the information are unleashed either like HIV/AIDS* into the intellectual anatomy of the recipient[2] or are let loose on the 'intellectual territories' of the recipient like the *demon-possessed-hell-encouraged 'soldiers' of ISIS and Boko-Haram*[3]; thereby messing up the recipient's mind with the resultant damages to his understanding of reality in that context [4]'(PAGovPat 5:1-4).

What?! Shush, calm down, Mr. and Mrs. 21st century, my dearest educated fools and informed simpletons. Don't hack me, don't, it is not my theory, it is the reality all around you, you spoilt and lazy-head generation. I am only codifying it so that you read and reflect if you still have that capacity!

Hence, being properly prepared to learn how to learn rightly and deduce correctly, not necessarily perfectly but correctly, from our ethnoreligious, socio-cultural and politico-economic relationships at various levels of our national life, opens a vista of possibilities (or power) that lie within us.

In other words, being properly 'educated and informed' enables us to see and believe that *education* is 'an on-going process for learning to learn correctly'. Consequently, this psychology equips us (the youths) with *the capacity* (or power or possibility) to see (almost) every unfaithful and manipulative step our psycharcinogenic leaders are stealthily taking, whether publicly or privately. It furnishes us with the *capacity* to discern the *anticipated* gains or losses of the 'high and low' political god-fathers, and to know what their god-sons fear most and what they are likely going to do to avert their most 'feared circumstances'.

Knowing and understanding those levels of relationships makes us free from their clutches to a reasonable extent and turn the chessboard around in our politico-economic matrix as a nation; thereby turning the chess players (i.e. the politicians and their cohorts) into the pawns (i.e. you and me) on the chessboard and the pawns into the chess players.

Please, bear in mind the fact that by saying 'properly informed or educated', I do not mean that we become 'psychics'[15]. That is, people who with a high degree of accuracy can anticipate, or in some cases, determine certain human actions or read people's mind without even seeing (the patients or victims or clients) those whose minds are being read, no, that is not my intention. Instead, I mean being mentally energetic and enthusiastic about knowing the truth provides the tools –tangible and mostly intangible- necessary for *chiselling out* the truth from of the *huge block of pure marble of reality* coated with 'rough edges of subtle but malicious fictions' created by the politicians and their cohorts.

These tools are all around us, and these tools are pieces of information we have accumulated over time and still accumulating rightly as they surface. These pieces of information have been *verified and then analyzed, re-analyzed and even over-analyzed* by different *agents of information dissemination* in (y)our environment. This process of information accumulation enhances our ability to read between the lines and helps us to know when our irrational parts are pushing us towards overlooking the danger inherent in the actions or inactions of public office holders, community leaders, religious leaders and, of course, anyone in our collective socio-economic and politico-cultural life's space.

What I am saying, in essence, is that if this generation is taking full advantage of all the opportunities available to it from education to information and communication technology and other areas that gravitate to it or it gravitates to, then this generation should be more at home with gathering general information about its environment which is natural thing to do for any 'processed-mind'. Thus, the disposition to gather information will enhance its sharpness, shrewdness and accuracy in reaching conclusions on germane issues of collective importance and, more particularly, this generation should be comfortable with gathering useful information about its socio-cultural and politico-economic conditions.

Also, this generation should be interested in getting and analyzing objectively any information about other players involved in its cultural-politico-economic conditions. Then use the analyzed pieces of information it gathers as the *knowledge base* from where it deduces informed and helpful points.

However, *the knowledge base* cannot and should not be used for rash, irrational and lazy-head conclusions that often make this generation or the majority of its members to 'switch off' their uninformed, and sadly, less sophisticated minds from receiving more mind-sharpening information from *credible sources that are available almost entirely free, nowadays.*

The *effects* of the inability of the members of this 'information-soaked' generation to challenge their brains and task their minds -by bending their heads to read meaningful materials that can aid them in their *self-discovery and the understanding of their place* in the scheme of things in their immediate environment thereby *engaging their minds in deeper reflections on what should have been in place but which has not-* are alarming, to say the least. The mental emptiness or intellectual lack of depth of huge percentage in/of this generation is sad, embarrassing and, somewhat, threatening to its future and that of its likely successors.

This generation or rather the majority of the members of this generation claim there is no difference between the politicians and the parties or the political associations they belong, *so,* they asked themselves rhetorically, *why do we have to worry about how our politics is run?*

Put differently, they (the members this emotive generation) say there is no need in attempting to filter the politicians and separate those with discernible genuine interest of the community at heart and with good public image (mind you, their image does not have to be perfect, and it ***will never be*** anyway) from those politicians that are not known to have any genuine interest of the community at heart, based on their antecedents, with their seemingly irredeemably tainted image, no matter how holy they now claim to be.

Yes, the best is what should be allowed to occupy all our *hallowed public offices*, but we can only select from those who have offered themselves or have been offered by others for service.

Let me digress a little by giving two unambiguous examples that should help you get a bit of the point I am making.

Digressing.....

First, Hilary F. Clinton of the Democratic Party and Donald J Trump of the Republican Party (GOP) were not the best candidates their respective parties could or should have thrown up for the 2016 presidential race. Neither were they the only ones in that November 2016 presidential race nor were they the best candidates the American society in its entirety could have produced in 2016, if they were the best in the real sense of it, then my honest thought was and is, that's an insult to the collective intelligence of the United States of America as a nation.

Yet, these two *morally bankrupt and disastrous and politically unpopular* candidates were the ones offered for service by the (elites') system controlled by the *two lungs* of all the political anatomy available in that nation, in spite of the fact that other parties –e.g. Libertarian and Green parties- exist on the edge of the American political landscape.

So, information-wise, it was up to the people to choose between (Mr. Trump and Mrs. Hilary) 'the *9/11 and Pearl Harbour or the devil and the deep blue sea' based* on what they were fed with by the compliant corporate media or what they chose to swallow as a people.

Second, Muhammadu Buhari of the All Progressives Congress and Goodluck Jonathan of the People Democratic Party were never and could not have been close to the best candidates Nigeria, a nation of about 190 million people, could throw up for March 2015 presidential election nor were they the economically most intelligent of all politicians and moneyticians available on the scene at that point in time. If they were, *then,* it's a shame on 1 out of every 10 black men on earth.

Nigeria with its huge intellectual class (home and abroad) can't convince me that those were the best potential-to-actual candidates in 2015.

But like in the case of USA 2016 presidential election, it was left for the people, the electorates, to de-emphasize or accentuate those hyper-emotive issues politicians were fond of throwing up in order to get into the corridors of power by manipulating everyone and exploiting us very well.

However, how do you vote rightly if you can't think outside the box? And how can you attempt thinking realistically when you haven't armed yourself with necessary mind sharpening information? Think about this for now, ok?

......Digression ended

Nevertheless, anyone who cannot show in his conducts or we cannot see in his antecedents that he has the interest of the community at heart does not deserve to occupy any public office, his holiness or sinfulness, real or imagined, notwithstanding.

Politicians are, no doubt, part and parcel of this society. And, as I said above, they are relational beings too; therefore, while there are things that elicit their interest, there are others that repel it within and outside the context of politics. Consequently, it will be erroneous for anyone in this emotive *generation* to say or claim that they are all the same and, so, there is no need for us to try to separate those who are *closer to what is desirable in political and public spheres,* based on their antecedents and what they currently represent, from those that *are closer to what is not desirable in political and public spheres,* judging by their antecedents, too, and what they currently stand for or represent.

Yes, generally, many people have evolved a cynical distrust of politicians, because of the insincerity of large hordes of politicians; maybe we cannot completely blame them for that distrust. This feeling of distrust is a universal relational phenomenon between politicians and the citizenry.

Yet, in any society where (especially young literate) people have not neglected the development of their minds and become unjustifiably lazy to read even the most minute but educative pieces of information that can liberate and elevate their minds, people don't just blindly lump all the politicians together in one brick. Even when it seems on the surface that almost every politician *lies* to get through, politically informed people still find time to gather and analyze information relating to particular individuals (or group of individuals), because they know that there are unifying (and/or distinguishing) factors that bring people of like minds together irrespective of how they are perceived by the general populace.

This *knowledge,* therefore, enables them to *pass informed judgment on the politicians' vote-worthiness or non-vote-worthiness.* In any case, they (the informed electorates) draw from the pool of undercurrent (i.e. privilege but revealed) information and current information (i.e. already in the public domains) in order *to wriggle or negotiate their way out of the seemingly dark mist of distrust covering their socio-political atmosphere.* And once the intellectual cum psychological foundation has been laid, and an informed and critical mind evolved, the structure of knowledge grows naturally effortlessly and, thus, the art of shrewd socio-political decision making becomes a graceful mental act; what will be needed later on is just to update the (data) knowledge constantly.

Unfortunately for a huge chunk of this generation (of which I am a member), rather than showing the strength of their rational minds or mental states on burning national issues as they affect their overall wellbeing by putting the politicians and other leaders on their toes for *their good and the overall good of Nigeria,* that is acting as the socio-economic-political sharpshooters, they go about saying: *money is all that matters and whoever brings money is the caring politician;* even if he does nothing meaningful with public resources *and swims in the ocean of corrupt practices.*

Thus, rather than being intellectually concerned with the socio-economic infrastructure that will bring about, in the short and long terms, an efficient and functional large-scale public systems, services, and facilities that are necessary for profitable local and national economic activities, including but not limited to meaningfully stable power and water supply, modern public transportation system, less-exploitative telecommunications system, good road networks, and genuine knowledge imparting and skills developing schools etc, they are preoccupied with stomach infrastructure, to borrow the popular phrase of Dr. Kayode Fayemi, the former Ekiti State governor and current minister of power and steel.

What do you expect from a supposedly privileged generation of the 21st century that lacks the most fundamental understanding of the principles of good *government and proactive governance* and the multi-directional effects of these on the state?

They, the members of this generation, forget or do know not that the worst form of poverty is not economic poverty but psycho-intellectual poverty! The poverty of the mind, a symbol of an infertile man or woman!

That is why as long as this generation go about with its lack of intellectual enthusiasm and vigor in addition to its tenacious superficial political morality, when it comes to carefully sifting socio-cultural, ethnoreligious and politico-economic issues affecting it and indeed the whole of the nation – notwithstanding, its involvement in 2015 general elections- this generation will always be a disaster of monumental category taking place or waiting to happen or emerge fully.

However, in Nigeria, my beloved country, a supposedly emerging modern economy in a modern state, the real sector of the economy, I will argue, is, regrettably, declining or waning with companies closing down or planning to fold up their productive activities every now and then within her boundaries and they are either relocating to other African countries or moving into non-existence altogether.

Chapter 13

THREE "MOST SUCCESSFUL" INDUSTRIES IN NIGERIA

(Politics, Proliferation of Religious Houses and Clustered Prostitution)

Every modern and genuine economy has two major sectors: the commercial sector and the real sector.

The commercial sector of the economy deals with distribution (not production) of goods and services. In other words, this sector of the economy is directly involved in the distribution of goods which have been produced or manufactured by the real (manufacturing) sector. Put differently, it deals with buying and selling of goods, and offering of services of varying degrees to clients (or customers); whether the services offered are (technical) skill-based or (general-ability) non-skill-based, all they do is to provide support for the clients (or customers) across the board in the economy of a particular state.

The second sector of the economy is the real sector; this is so-called because it is responsible for manufacturing or production of goods to be distributed (and serviced) by the other sectors of the economy. This sector of the economy produces everything from the simplest products such as ordinary tooth-pick and toothbrush packs to complex devices such as mobile phones, laptops, or machines such as cars, aeroplanes etc.

Simply put, the manufacturing or the real sector of the economy is the foundation of any genuinely strong modern economy.

Thus, every sane nation across the world constantly conceives, designs and develops industrial strategies that can aid the emergence of this all-important aspect of their economy and sustain its survival, development and growth.

……..Digressing……

Fundamentally speaking, the so-called Donald J Trump's trade *resetting* with China, aka Sino-American trade war seasons 1 & 2, was essentially about what?

Apart from the political undertones, it was because both nations know that the powers inherent in the real sector of a modern economy are immense and depleting or losing this real sector is like losing one of their lungs, I mean economically.

………Digression ended….

Therefore, the real sector of the economy is very important, even if it produces only the most basic products that meet the daily needs of the people. For instance, products like tissue papers; tooth-picks; tubes of toothpaste; cutleries and so on, may look simple but people need them. So irrespective of the simplicity of the manufacturing sector, it nonetheless injects a certain level of powerful and cost-effective stability into the socio-political cum economic fibres of any political entity that embraces it.

However, here in Nigeria, my beloved country, a supposedly emerging modern economy and a modern state, the real sector of the economy, *I will argue,* is, regrettably, declining or waning with companies closing down or folding up their productive activities within her boundaries. In other words, they are either relocating to other African countries with more stable power supply or moving into non-existence altogether[1].

However, our waning and dilapidating manufacturing industries notwithstanding, there are other emerging industries, though they squarely fall into the commercial sector of the economy – buying and selling and offering of services. But the following are my 'snap focus' here in this chapter: politics, the proliferation of religious houses and prostitution[2].

These 3Ps are actually 'employing' a sizeable number of our people in different ways and manners. I do not claim to have any detailed statistics on or about the extent of the employment provided by these *three ludicrous informally-formal industries,* and I am sure the government (state and federal) themselves do not have any detailed statistics, why, because they don't even know how many *special assistants* to their special assistants they pay their absurd salaries.

Did you say this is crazy? No, it is not crazy it de-most-crazy, that is, it is a demonstration of the neurotic madness of a state in the cloak of civil rule or, if wish, in the garment of democracy!

The Political Industry

Though politics in *any sane* country or society anywhere in the world is a serious business, for the most part, it is for serious minded people. In other words, is it is a vocation or an endeavour for conscientious and trustworthy people whose sole or overriding interest is what they can give to their nation for its growth and development through visionary and invaluable leadership style that is committed to the greater good of the largest possible number of people in the short term and the overall good of all in the long term.

Note that I am not saying there are no parasitic politicians anywhere else in the world except here. Instead, what I am saying is that where sanity prevails in the polity, the public officials and/or policies do not focus on what their country can give to them through humongous salary structure and other everlastingly-hilarious entitlements and benefits at the detriment of the people of such state.

Here in my beloved motherland, however, politics is a huge money-spinning industry in our economy.

The understanding of politics as a business in Nigeria is not in the technical sense of it being an endeavour for people who are selflessly-focused and determined to bring forth the progress of a particular political entity or state, rather it is taken in the literal sense of it being a commercial dealing though it produces or manufactures nothing that can directly be bought or sold by the people of Nigeria.

Yet it generates unimaginable wealth and associated powers and, of course, it generates employment opportunities for some cronies and cronies' cronies. That is the interesting thing about it!

Many of our companies are folding up or have folded up due to none availability of power supply or owing to its erratic existence as the chief reason because the cost of production was and is unmanageably and frustratingly high. Why, because they have to power their factories for production for days running into weeks and, in some cases, weeks running into months while using, in most cases, diesel-powered generators. This was and is an unforgivable 'forced' commercial-suicide for many of the business owners.

Consequently, tens of thousands running into hundreds of thousands were (and are being) laid off by such disappearing and/or already disappeared companies thereby increasing the army of the qualified but unemployed people and, hence, generating more materials for manipulation or anarchy in the hands of our deranged-angels or civilized-demons wearing well-starched *agbada* and parading themselves as occupiers of our public offices.

Fortunately for the political industry in Nigeria, unlike all other industries whether extinct, existing or trying to exist, it does not need electricity to run its core business of swindling the Nigerian state of its God-given wealth.

Unlike our failing manufacturing industries and struggling service-oriented commercial entities that need electricity more than life itself, politics in Nigeria does not bother 'its head' about availability or non-availability of electricity since it does not need it to, like a vampire, suck the financial blood of Nigeria and Nigerians. It does not need it to strip the country naked of the dignity providence has endowed it by swimming in the ocean of every form of corrupt practices.

It does not need it to act with impunity and blatant disregard for the rule of law; however, like the possessed Roman emperor Nero, our 'inverted politics' does need the absence of electricity to rule over a republic that is *violently burning with the wildfires of poverty and* underdevelopment.

Simply put, politics, as commonly practised in Nigeria, *has our holistic development as its remotest concern,* if it had any concern for us at all. So electricity is the least of our politicians' interest; their political survival is their preoccupation since this assures them of a steady flow of money, power and privilege!

Given that our politicians do not see electricity as an indispensable driver of modern industrialized economy which can and will, in the short term, reduce the number of the unemployed and, in the long term, decrease the territory poverty already had carved out of our motherland, therefore, they really don't care about making it work. Never be deceived by their political face-saving talks about their concerns about our near-dead power sector and fake zeal to transform it and make it work. It is a lie. They have been saying that since I was born. Now I am writing about it.

And if perchance, they know the effects of stable power supply on the economy of this country, and yet they choose to ruin us or our economy for their gutter and damned self-interests, then they are eternal embers from the pits of hell!

I or rather we and our more fearsome intellectual offspring shall squeeze and liquidate you and your families one day, very soon.

It's a matter of time, we shall achieve that and it will be peaceful, legal, generally supported but disastrous for you and your abominable inheritors. It's a promise and it shall be fulfilled, I have nothing to lose anymore, you bastards took it already, now I live for the good of others and this is better.

Do not live to see the day of your dispossession because, seeing your fate, Sodom and Gomorra will thank God for their fates.

In any case, seeing that in our political industry there is no risk of having to burn (millions in purchase of) diesel day and night to produce goods or products that may not even bring encouraging short-term profits or that may not be accepted generally by the consumers for a while, every class of privileged-idiots, educated-morons, successful-failures, refurbished-lunatics and liberated-thick-skin-robbers now populate the political territory hunting for treasure day and night.

They, like Lassa-fever carrying rats, infest our nation with life-threatening ailments that inflict economic muscle pains, moral ulcers of the ethical mucous membranes, social headaches, population haemorrhage, and psychological, cultural and spiritual heart and kidney failure to this country.

They, like demons called gas flaring, pollute the air with different kinds of paralyzing gases causing damages to our economic-political environment.

These empty-head politicians turn the whole politics of this nation into a gold mine, and they have never stopped mining and excavating our economic treasures illegally and carelessly. With this greed of theirs, they have done much damage done to our national socio-cultural environment: our economic disciplines, our public morals and social ethics. Their aim is power, money and privileges (PMP) and, these they get at every successful excavation, I mean whenever they *capture powers of the state* and loot our treasuries, our commonwealth.

The deep well of wealth available in this country, from the top to the bottom of our political hierarchy, is like a bowl of moistened-sugar in a flies-infested neighbourhood, attracting everyone; man and woman of stout greed and skills-for-illegal-wealth-hunting.

Hence, the industry of politics boasts of the higher number of rich(est) men and women when compared with the other industries combined. Of course, in reality, the richest men and women in Africa, and particularly in Nigeria, are ex or serving (ruling) politicians. Even though all these politicians will never admit it, nonetheless, they know it is true.

This is an industry heavily populated with or by professional politicians, although we are now having some *professionals making a stifled* inroad into the political terrains of this country. Yet, it seems evident that they (i.e. the professionals) are either suffering from the same collective moral-bankruptcy, a bug that is increasingly dominating our life as a nation, or they *lack the discipline and dedication* to effect the change that is meaningful and commendable or their number as the 'selfless ones' is so small that they are only existing on *the margin of the political notebook* of this nation, and it may as well be the combination of all the conditions mentioned above.

Whichever way you want to look at it, one thing that is conspicuously undeniable in Nigeria's industry of politics (i.e. moneytics) is the fact that political opportunists, illegal-wealth-hunters, successful-failures, educated-morons[3], privileged-simpletons[4], refurbished-lunatics[5] and liberated-thick-skin-robbers[6] and the likes now populate the political territory hunting for treasure day and night. For these hordes, no business or job that can assure them of the degree of powers, money and privileges available in the political industry in Nigeria as facilitated by their political companies erroneously called 'parties'.

Therefore, their most favoured political scriptural quotation is found in *the satirical book of* Pathological Attachment to Government Patronage chapter one verse one to three (or PAGovPat 1:1-3) and it says:

"Seek yee first the powers of any of the levels of government of the flawed and counter-productive Nigeria political system and every undeserved, unmerited, unearned and unjustified economic and social privileges shall be added automatically [1]. For no one really cares about who you are but what you are and have [2]. No one really wants to know how you get what, what they care about is if you have got the powers to explore and exploit the wealth of the state [3]."

As a result, almost every one of these politicians is a 'businessman', or privilege-monetizer and they love meditating on their possessed inspirational Machiavellian principle (i.e. as found in the satirical Pagovpat Chapter 2:1-2), which says:

"...just a little investment with proper political calculations and the returns on the investments will be in the thousands, and millions -overwhelming[1]; and at the appropriate time in the game of deceit and counter-deceits and betrayal of trust billions will roll in and a boss you, too, shall be" [2].

Nothing expresses their sick governing propensity more than this *satirical scripture Pagovpat* text above. Of course, not all politicians are evil-manipulators, thieves and deceivers; there are amazingly moral and ethical politicians here and there, that is a fact, too.

Politics of Investment with Huge Returns

Just before 2015 general elections, there were certain media reports that some politicians were selling some of their houses[7] and other landed properties in places like Port Harcourt, Abuja and Lagos etc., to finance their political interests.

Though it might be mere speculation and it might be real, but in all honesty I was not surprised to hear that it was brought up in the media, because in our immediate environment we all know the type of investments, if I may call it that, which certain politicians make in order to gain even marginal powers so as to boost their egos as local champions. Even if the reports were 30% true, two things can at least be deduced from the said reports.

First many politicians have soft spots for gaining power at all cost and the politicians involved in the so-called property sale were either without 'generous' godfathers who were willing to risk footing the entire bill(s) from their personal purses and get their lion-share returns if the venture was successful; such godfathers have always been with us after all. Have they not?

Second, it might be that the politicians involved in the alleged property sale were not ready to bend to any one's edicts in case they capture the much cherished politico-economic treasures of their territory and, so, they were willing to break through the political brick walls all alone at any cost and quadruple their possessions, powers and privileges, after any successful charge-through or eventual victory.

While I am not claiming to possess any hard fact about those media reports, I, however, speculatively speaking, think those reported cases of house sales might be 'true' after all, tell me why would anyone want to spend between N3,000,000 to N27, 000,000[8] on mere nomination form in a large but shrinking economic condition of 2014/2015 election season? Well, food for future thoughts.

We have seen how people became ordinary councillors in our neighbourhoods, and after just about two years they are buildings houses and buying cars that show certain levels of sudden wealth, though it may not be huge but surprising all the same because we know them very well before hitting the Nigeria treasure land –politics. And there were some who became millionaires within that same period just because they hunted at a level higher than mere councillorship positions and while some others just became inexplicably rich within a year or two of diving into office.

Employment Strategies

Well, irrespective of what the real reason(s) beneath the surface of the alleged sales of politicians' landed properties might be a few months to the 2015 general elections in which the politicians in question or their cronies were participants, it was nothing but a reflection of what happens daily in the beneath-the-scene world of our politics.

One thing is certainly common in every political part of this huge republic, Nigeria's political terrain has become a 'treasure hunting ground' and, people will do anything to acquire a portion of this treasure-rich-territory (of politics) in order to ensure that they have a share of the seemingly inexhaustible commonwealth of (Nigerians and) Nigeria.

Meanwhile, many of these empty-heads turned-privileged-personalities, popularly but mistakenly called politicians, even before they win any public office, are fond of rashly committing themselves to extreme promises. They weave a fabric of gullible followers whom they promise one unrealistic thing or the other, should they, the foot soldiers –i.e. their supporters, walk on razor-edge bare-footed for their success at the polls.

For instance, the alleged perpetrators of the Thursday, April 5th, 2018, bank robbery[9] in Offa, Kwara state confessed to being (former?) political thugs who relied on crumbs from the tables of both Senate president Dr Bukola Saraki (APC) and the governor of the state, Alhaji Abdulfatah Ahmed (APC). Of course, I believe they didn't rob banks on the orders of these prominent moneyticians. Nevertheless, they claimed they once worked as thugs for them; that was what the lead robber claimed, probably true.

If the armed robbers' claims were true, then we can safely infer that those robbers were once protected by the politicians in question, perhaps unknowingly. Well, let the real Nigerian investigative journalists do their best to uncover the truth.

Anyway, for politicians to create a job for 'the boys', on assumption of office, they create phantom offices upon offices to *feed the boys* (and girls too). Consequently, needless commissions, agencies and committees are set up to empower and remunerate their foot soldiers, families-and-friends, concubines and other supportive bootlickers *in mufti and uniforms.*

The manner with which they do this (phantom office creation) suggests they once worked with the devil in the inner chamber of hell where *greed, deceptions and lies are expertly manufactured* every *metaphysical-nanosecond that beats the watchful eyes of even the most alert Angel on guard.*

With these empty heads in drivers' seat, they choose special advisers to aid their none-existent skills in (statecraft) driving. These special advisers (SAs) employ personal assistants (PAs), then PAs will have secretaries to personal assistants (SPAs) and their secretaries will have their special aids (SAs), too; by employing personal assistants or whatever the title they are given, the list is so multifarious that, secretly, they seem to be intentionally confusing us with titles or arrogantly harassing us openly with them.

In any case, they provide jobs for the boys at the expense of running an effective system of government that can define and be a template or model for infrastructural development that will open the length and breadth of Nigeria to ferocious but ordered holistic development which could make Nigeria, my country, *a true beacon of hope* for the Black World!

Proliferation of Religious Houses

I wonder how many religious houses with different moribund doctrines or confused economic-crisis-driven doctrines are to be found in each of our neighbourhoods across this republic.

Of course, the so-called western world has many weird independent religious organizations too, even some with weirder beliefs and ways of life[10], but the west is not my headache here, Nigeria is. So, if you, the reader, can attempt a census of the religious houses in your neighbourhood, especially if you dwell in a city or urban area, you will be amazed at how many religious houses claim allegiance to a particular religion but without any direct or indirect relationship with one another; in fact, they are usually involved in what I call client-raiding[11].

The more the economic conditions bite, the more the proliferation of houses of worship we experience. The 'god' of these religions must be a real smart being. Judging by the claims of those putting up and managing these religious houses, that god must have called them, otherwise, they won't be in the business of gathering people for religious services. Wow! What a smart being is this god of theirs!

This god is so smart that in his unrivalled retarded wisdom he's covering the clumsiness of a nation, as reflected by its lethargic leadership class, with religious mushrooms and leeches of different religious titles; also in his everlasting retrogressive intelligence he's replacing manufacturing companies that can transform the whole society to a more stable and rationally progressive one with a vastly emotive religious bodies which, for the *most* part, have greed for *power, money and fame* as their governing propensities, and, thereby making the society less economically stable, less open to progressive development and more open to delusional view of religion, life and the true GOD.

I do not think we can forget Boko Haram delusions[12] quite easily! Can we? Even if we, in our usual pathetic national-partial-amnesia (i.e. limited collective memory-loss) forget, Borno state and the whole of poverty and violence wrecked North-east, especially Chibok town, will NEVER forget!

There are millions of Nigerians swimming in the real and nauseating ocean of poverty, in spite of the huge wealth of Nigeria. This is due to the availability of only a handful of reasonably dignifying employment opportunities in the country for a large number of qualified, able and willing Nigerians –old and young. The scanty employment opportunities are the result of the *malignant incompetence* of our ruling elites, especially since May 29, 1999[13] - the beginning of the fourth republic.

There seems to be the need to give hope to the hopeless millions of this nation and save them from the evil-infested ocean of poverty, for this reason there emerged (and are still emerging) a collections of religious houses with different spiritual claims; both outrageous ones and genuine ones share the same space -Nigeria. They emerged in order to offer services and fees are paid without being charged[14].

Well, they started timidly but now they are bold and even bullish in their activities nowadays. Many of them are religious in name but the services they offer or they claim to offer depict them as *substitutes to certain failed or failing agencies of the state*. One will not really be surprised if they actually replace some agencies of the state in some sense because the uselessness of many of government agencies is nasty!

Anyway, proliferation of religious houses or spiritual groups is so successful that we might very soon, if the decay in this country's economy and educational sector continues, have a religious meeting point in every house; after all, almost every street in any modern Nigerian city is a host to a church/ prayer centre or a mosque/ an Ala-Saalatu group[15].

The increase in the religious cum spiritual business activities has actually created wonderful employment opportunities for many. In fact, the glory and honour of being a pastor or imam, for example, is so huge that every misfit of the society wants to bear and carry religious titles such as pastor, apostle, prophet, evangelist, reverend, bishop, deacon, father, imam, sheik, alfa, guru, maharishi etc.

This business of marketing religion, that is religionomics, is a huge empire that covers different religions within Nigeria's economic boundaries. This religious business grows every day because the negative economic weights are crushing the rational strength of many and rapidly depleting the 'ozone-layer' of their hope, thereby exposing their lives or minds to the unhealthy 'ultraviolet radiation' of poverty.

Consequently, the number of people earnestly seeking refuge in the religious offices or houses or shops or clinics from harsh economy-induced problems of varying degrees is ever-increasing, even education *seems* not to be making any difference in the manner people rush to these supposed safe-havens. Why, because education itself is experiencing the quaking economy of the nation, and thus its qualities nowadays seem to be evaporating, at least that is my candid opinion.

Whether you like what I am pointing out or not, you cannot deny the fact that religion is now really a big business (in Nigeria) and it is employing a lot of people, even though a huge chunk of the people it employs are its (religion) involuntary employees.

Put differently, some people would have preferred other jobs but chose religious service because it saves them from poverty; or put mildly, religion has been forced to employ millions, directly or indirectly, whom it has no need of or people who have no worth for the projects of religion itself – saving souls and protecting them from the wolf packs.

In any case, religion has assumed dramatic features that make one wonder if it is now genuinely concerned with its core spiritual and humanitarian goals. Whenever you listen to advertisements of religious events or programmes, one hears service descriptions that are prevalent in other economic sectors of the Nigerian society, I mean it is like they are advertising refined herbal products or Vitalo or Maclean tooth paste etc.

For example, the radio airwaves are always bombarded with different bogus claims of different religious houses or groups saying that if you attended their programme the visa 'blockage' you are experiencing will be removed instantly; and if you have been looking for a job for a long time, the doors of job opportunities will be opened instantly (or leseke'ese). Or if you have university admission problems, by attending their so-called spiritual programmes, admission become a possibility for you. In fact, there are many other ridiculous advertisements that reveal the underlining business instincts of the so-called spiritual matters.

This version of religion is opening more elitist schools than necessary, the majority of medium-sized religious organizations that have their own elitist-styled schools. Let get something clear here, it is not that founding or owning a school is bad or evil or immoral, no, never. But the aims of running many of these schools, whose quality is mostly found on the sign-posts, not in the classrooms, are largely reflected in their outrageous school fees that make them look and act more elitist, and this is what I challenge.

For instance, how many of the schools owned by religion-based organizations can openly boast of having the children of a less-buoyant citizen, I mean a member of their (own) congregation whose tithes contributed to the school's existence, on their active register of enrolled students?

However, unlike the political sector of the economy that does not need electricity to operate, religion, a non-productive sector, needs electricity more than the politicians do; of course, not in the manner a real manufacturing industry needs it for production. Nevertheless, since the erratic supply of power by all our 'Discos', i.e. the power utility companies, affects the churches and mosques too, generators are there to provide the energy they will need to power their noise-making mountain-top mega speakers at little or no cost to the cleric in charge. After all, members of the congregation can always supply that or god will supply it through the 'miracle seeking fools'.

With countless religious organizations across the federation, job generation by the 'religious industry' has increased, and people who felt it was wise to work for religion and religion-related goals are being employed by religion. In other words, those who think that religion can be used to achieve their goals in life, no matter how heinous the goals are, have been manipulating religion! Our religious life that should be a living documentary for people to watch, *in order to see the beauty of the divine in understandable human reality* has, sadly, become an award-winning mockumentary[16].

Nevertheless, religion is an important aspect of human experience, and, as long as a human being remains a dualistic being, he will always find a reason to commune with his creator(s), and this will always ensure the existence of religion.

However, when there are too many 'creators and objects' of worship, as we have in Nigeria today, and other (poverty infested) regions of the world, spiritual slavery and deception will always ensure that emotion push analytic or structured reasoning to the background and what we get in return is stagnation or disordered economic growth or dead-slow progressive development; that is if there are semblances of development to start with. Thus, we must always bear in mind that e*motion without reason ruins vision even before its realization process begins.* Where has emotive religion led us as a nation?

Prostitution

Prostitution is a complex issue and a universal phenomenon. It is a very ancient-modern business, and it can be very confusing, sometimes, when trying to examine it in any society. Well, in actual fact I am not treading a new path here but an old path in a new context.

Hence, I won't even dissipate my energy on this at all because *it's a familiar guest that kisses our daily reality 'right cheek'* as a nation in various forms: from the religious institutions to the political, financial to educational etc,.

A move around major streets of any of our important or even less important cities in Nigeria at masked-hours (the dark periods) of the day will give you the idea of the sordid business going on across the federation in the (bright-hours) 'bare face' hours of the day behind hundreds of thousands of corporate and individual business activities.

There are students who run two-degree programmes at the same time: one academic and the other prostitution. We have marketers of different companies reaching out to clients or customers in manners not too different to brothel workers. The banking sector, however, leads the way in exploiting Nigerians, young women especially, for corporate prostitution.

When these ladies got their jobs, they were happy they were leaving the *High school of the Unemployed* and gaining admission into the *University of the Employed.* However, but no sooner had they resumed their duty posts than they realized that, dining with the devil requires a long sturdy spoon of cold, old, bold tricks[17].

These corporations select beautiful ladies, ladies who ordinarily would have preferred other jobs than sitting behind the cashier desk 8 am to 5 pm Monday to Friday or hunting for prospective (mostly male) customers, customers whom they would rather not want know in their lives.

These banks go for ladies with 'powerful body assets'; assets in their 'past' and their 'future'[18], that's weapon of mass attraction, assets that make it difficult for men, men whose moral integrity seems to drop below zero degrees every day, to resist transacting business with the bank those ladies represent.

The term of the transaction is simple: you transact with my bank to hit my target, I lay your bed. Shush! It is called marketing not what you are thinking, don't be a dirty-minded reader.

I can only laugh it out in Greek. Well, there is a saying that in an open-air religious crusade, *there is no need for long sermons in a hot summer afternoon,* just hit the point, and the hearers get the message. It is cold-funny, I mean it's a hilarious absurdity, yet it is a continuous reality, nonetheless.

Of course, the banking sector merely leads the way in trading *juicy evelyn flesh* for the business transaction of the customers' accounts. It is not as though they are the only institution involved in the corporate abuse of Nigerians, especially through the promotion of 'corporate prostitution', by manipulating and exploiting the fears of their (female) employees. Unfortunately, it is just one popular example.

Nigeria is an interesting country in which anything happens. Properly put in the Nigerian style, I will say this 'na Kontiry wey everytin goes….'

Chapter 14

NIGERIA'S MAJOR 'IMPERIAL' ELITES

(Economic-terrorist, political- billionaires and the men of goodies)

Nigeria is an interesting country in which anything happens. Properly put in the Nigerian style, I will say *this 'na kontry wey everytin goes....'*

Here in my beloved country, Nigeria, we are told that we are free from the sick British colonialism/imperialism –a sort of legitimized thievery. Fine, congrats for the freedom! But what's the difference, when we are now held captives by lots of human pests and parasites? That is to say, we, the people, have now, to some extent, become the personal property of a bunch of *unfortunate-misfits that control the political and economic* live wires of our wealthy-but-poor country, and, they are always ready to disconnect the energy-current of life from the source for this nation whenever it suits their 'hellish desires'.

There are a lot of things or persons holding us back but here are three most powerful of these forces: economic-terrorists, political-billionaires and the so-called men of god – the MoGs.

The bondage of Nigeria and Nigerians are being sustained by these groups and their beneficiaries. They walk hand in hand and hand in glove, whether they think it, show it and know it or not, the pattern is always there for the discerning minds to see.

These are groups of men and women who rule Nigeria from the corner of their offices or places of operation, their only gains are *wealth, fame and power*. I think this class of rogue power grabbers and controllers-behind-the-scene are called 'deep state' in other parts of the world -e.g. the US, but I think they are *deeper-state* in here in Nigeria.

If in any election they decided to support 'Mr. Lucifer' himself, it will take the extraordinary ***active*** participation of our peoples *mental, emotional* and *physical* '**wills'** and the *grace* of the real God, not let them succeed. Unfortunately, many of us are still dangerously tied to the apron of irrational sentiments that prevent us from seeing beneath the surface of what they present to us.

Economic-Terrorists

Who is a terrorist? A terrorist might easily be described as someone that uses naked violence, which might take the forms of bombing, kidnapping, and assassination to intimidate people, often for gaining political control of a state or an entity or to get what he (through his gang) demands from a government.

Thus, an economic-terrorist in this context is anyone who manipulates economic dealings to perpetrate financial violence on the people of a state, or an entity, whether covertly or overtly, in order to gain huge financially advantageous strength that makes him attractive to the ever-greedy politicians[1] in *corridors of power*. Consequently, when he is courted by the politicians his power and fame swell because a give-and-take relationship –quid quo pro- is established.

The economic-terrorists are those midnight-businessmen who are not, overtly, politicians but often than not have a certain level of alliance with the politicians and so they are shrewdly protected by the politicians in the corridors of power. They enjoy the tactful political 'umbrella' and economic 'fountains'[2] that make them wealthier while they covertly short-*change the people of the state in their economic dealings* with the full knowledge of the public officeholders.

In fact, without mentioning anyone of them in particular, you can easily know them if you are one of those who follow current public issues in this country or anywhere else. Are you having a mental collection of names and pictures of those who might be in this powerful group already?

Let me peel off the rind of your memory about the events of the recent past. About six years ago, there was the issue of subsidy[3] scam that got weird and wild under the administration or government of Dr. Goodluck Jonathan. So, the House of the Representatives probed the scam, while the probe was somewhat soiled by Mr. Farouk Lawal's disappointing *long-throat,* a couple of persons were, nonetheless, indicted for being allegedly involved in the fuel subsidy scam. And, unsurprisingly, one of the major persons whose names were mentioned was Femi Otedola, the chairman of Forte Oil. He was, at the time, one of the important 'angles' of the PDP (the then ruling gang) eminent 'poly-angles' of financiers.

Do you remember that? Well, what happened later? Nothing. Hmmn! I guess the rest is history now.

There are many economic terrorists in Nigeria, just as you will find them in any country, especially in an unserious country where individuals are stronger than the state. Go east, west, north and south; they are everywhere. And their number seems to increase by the tick of the clock.

For instance, at a time in the history of this country, especially between years 2000 and 2007, a particular businessman named Aliko Dangote, a major financier of the then ruling PDP (well, Dangote never hid the fact that he was their financier or one of their financiers), was widely rumored (or reported?) to have been granted the *express permission*[4] to be the only one to import sugar and rice for the whole nation for a certain period of time[5].

If that was true, which likely was, then, it probably was a sort of discreet alliance between the guard (Olusegun Obasanjo was the president in power then between 1999-2007) hired *to protect a dairy farm (where dairy cows were being carefully bred)* and a milk-thief. The thief scaled the fence and milked the cows secretly while the guard looked the other way, claiming ignorance of the thievery. This was not uncommon in Nigeria, anyway. Thus, without announcement, the thief knows what to do when the proceeds of their dirty dealings started tumbling in.

The economic-terrorists are not interested in the development of the state wealth, although they always pretend to be the collaborators-in-development (C-in-D) with the state, or whoever was handling the state affairs. However, they are nothing but culprits-in-stagnation-and-underdevelopment (C-in-SU). Thus, their sole interest has always been to challenge and undermine *the supremacy of the sanctity of our commonwealth* by manipulating the laws and ordinances that protect it. Consequently, they stop at nothing in their efforts to short-change the state and its people in business dealings. I mean they sell our state properties to themselves using crooked laws, NEPA is a vivid example.

They don't destroy the state; they simply steal its wealth. So that it exists for them, defends their interests and depends on them. Why? Because money can be used to lure the lawmakers, law enforcers and law itself away from their doorsteps, thereby becoming some sort of *law-unto-themselves*.

Consequently, the doors of impunity of socio-economic dominance will be left open. Who will check the guards when the guards are *irredeemably and morally* defective and corrupt?

I remember vividly, about three weeks (or thereabouts) after the March 28, 2015, presidential and national assembly elections, a dark cloud of fuel scarcity was concocted by some known and unknown economic-terrorists. So, by the last week of April stroke first week of May 2015, the 'acid rains' of fuel scarcity began to rain with a ferocity that threatened the joy of most humble and even rich Nigerians. As if that was not enough, where the fuel was available for sale, with few exceptions, it was sold for as high as N150 per litre in the first two weeks of the acidic rains of scarcity foisted on the nation by the *economic-terrorists* and their collaborators in government who lacked state management mentality and social skills but very *adept in the science of thievery* or looting of state resources and related science.

When the heinous fuel scarcity entered third and fourth weeks respectively, *the testicles of the nation were squeezed harder* and with malignant intents. so, the petrol was sold for as high N350 per litre in parts of Lagos, for instance, and even here in Ibadan!

So, who gained from that unchecked madness foisted on the nation by the economic-terrorists, their commanders and their foot soldiers[6]?

Who? We the citizens, or the government or none of us or all of us; or the marketers?

And who was the loser? Nigeria was, literally, brought to its knees, especially in the third and fourth week of the atrocious game of scarcity respectively, while billions of naira were squeezed out of the already hyper-squeezed pockets of millions of Nigerians, yet a seriously impotent government only watched absent-mindedly preoccupied with nothing in particular but character emptiness, managerial calamity, foresight erosion, hindsight collapse, introspection distortion.

In short, the government was in a vegetative state that has been its trademark since its inception on May 29, 2011.

Whether it was intentional or not, the incompetence of the government, back then, allowed the economic terrorists to strike in manners that showed that the phantom subsidy was merely a smokescreen for financial cum economic arm-twisting and, violation of the Nigerian state and its blessed population by these insane slaves naira turned rulers.

We are now in 2018, and 2019 is knocking at the door, but has anything changed? Has the government become more proactive instead of being ridiculously reactive?

Or just as president Trump of the Republican Party in the USA complains about Obama disasters every day, instead of doing his bit, is Buhari still crying about the ruinous Jonathan tenure?

Or is APC, now fully in power, still moaning over the ruins of *Jonathanian* PDP? Leave the 'poor' man alone and do your work. Even the professor of idiots knows that the *Jonathanian administration,* sentiments aside, nose-dived the economy of Nigeria, whether innocently or ignorantly, who cares, he did it that's all. Mrs Okonjo-Iweala (former 'minister' of Finance) would even attest to that quite easily.

However, I would say without mincing words that, it is nothing short of irresponsibility and lack of imagination for APC/Buhari to sit in the PDP/Jonathanian past, instead of analyzing *its (i.e. PDP/Jonathanian) successes and failures and use* the synthetic result of that analysis for projecting more accurately for our tomorrow and move on; only looking back once in a while to see if you are doing worse or better.

Political-Billionaires

Who is the richest man in Nigeria? Is he a businessman or a politician? Generally, though I have my reservation about that, the richest man in Nigeria is believed to be a businessman, and they say he is

Aliko Dangote. For real? Who knows that may be true, and it may be the most outrageous lie of our time, I suppose it is more of the latter.

What is the true financial worth of each of any of our living major public office holders- former or present? Who knows? Well, maybe in the future he, Dangote, is going to be the richest man in Nigeria or Africa or wherever his wealth will truly make him the heaviest man in town. But in reality if we can see a seriously fearless leader who can question the covert and overt economic templates of Nigerian 'wealth-hawkers' (the so-called political businessmen) you will be amazed by what you will see. You will, embarrassingly, discover that the richest man in Nigeria is a politician, and a huge or the highest number of billionaires we have in Nigerian reside in the 'political estate' built by free state money by polithiefians and, not the business estate built majorly with *shrewdness, sweats, accountability and perseverance of genuine businessmen* who invested their time and hard-earn money properly.

Who are political-billionaires? These are *tainted professional politicians who help themselves with state resources for as long as they have access to them.*

They –the political-billionaires- may be richer than 'sekere'[7] before getting into the public office, and they may simply be a little *richer than the church mouse* as at the time they assumed the office, whichever is applicable. The point, however, is that by the time they leave the office they would have become exceedingly rich, richer than the state treasury from which they have stolen by perforating it with scythe-like pens.

These people are found in all Nigeria's political parties, such as PDP, APC, LP, DPP, NNPC, EFCC, NPA, FAAN, NANS, , SSS, NPF, MTM, CAN,NCIA, BON etc. Wait a minute, did I say parties? Anyway, parties if what we currently have in Nigeria can be thus called, after all any idiot can float anything in the cloak of a party.

Although these state parasites (political billionaires) flaunt their wealth, yet they are quite smart about the details of their wealth; they conceal the details as much as possible. Why, because they know that if the details of their ill-gotten economic status become a public knowledge and an ingredient of public debate there is the possibility that they *might lose some level* of support, security and acceptability in their immediate environment, especially if they are from western Nigeria where the people have that political consciousness to somewhat question their suspicious leaders by lessening their influence through grass-root castigation of whatever they stand for -good or bad.

Thus, many of them 'set up' companies by proxies and pump part of their ill-gotten wealth into such chimpanzee companies. And having set up such companies, they do everything possible to scout for government patronage for them, using every connection they have to get it done. Thereby establishing rich *safe haven* for their money or rather our money stolen by them, and also using the companies as the superb conduit pipes for pumping away state resources into different *discreet but gaping* accounts across the Atlantic ocean in manners that reminds one of the crimes of trans-Atlantic slave trade that took place between 17th to 19th centuries.

These accounts are always expectant, like the miserable white farmers in their abominable monstrous hell called farms across the Atlantic Ocean during the evil era of slave trade. They (the gaping accounts) await financial captives of the political billionaires to secretly sail the ocean to the banks (modern farms for the enslaved-money from African economies) on 'the other side of the ocean'.

These political-billionaires are powerful people who always have one leg in government and one leg in business. They are shrewd people when it comes to stealing and deceit; however, they lack the required expertise for state management. Of course, to be fair to them, there is a marginal percentage among them that possess the rare gift of being astute *state managers and treasury looters* at the same time.

Hmm! What a gifted few! They control the economic destiny of this country; they influence the direction of the decision of drivers of the state affairs, whether it favours the general populace or not as long as it pleases them and their accursed desires then it is right, especially if the man in the driver's seat is a gifted inept and clueless leader-dealer[8].

Some of these wretched hordes are even richer than some countries on the continent of Africa. Yet, they will never be listed as being among the *richest treasury perforators* or empty-heads or thieves in Nigeria in particular, and on the African continent in general by any of those wealth-obsessed magazines of European and American origins.

Who knows the actual worth of our ex-governors before and after their tenure of office: from Godwill Akpabio of Akwa Ibom to Sani Yerima of Zanfara; from Tinubu of Lagos to Orji Uzor Kalu of Abia; and from Saraki Bukola of Kwara to infamous James Ibori of Delta? What about Ladoja and Alao-Akala of Oyo state?

Note that as political-billionaires they want to hold on to the politico-economic powers always, which they enjoy. Therefore, anything that will threaten the goodwill which the people in their immediate environment shower on them and, which calm their nerves somewhat, must be avoided by all means.

Hence they put up a false personality with the sole aim of deceiving the public –the people, their constituents. A couple of ex-public office holders that have been prosecuted or are being prosecuted, though with kid gloves, especially former governors such as Bode George, late Deprieye Alamesieya, Ayo Fayose, Alao-Akala, Gbenga Daniel, James Ibori, Lucky Igbinedion, Rasheed Ladoja, Diezani Alison-Madueke, Sambo Dasuki to name but a few, have proven this fact.

In any case, one thing is certain, and that is, these people, these political billionaires are both openly and tacitly ruling and controlling this country, either as a conscious group of cabals[9] or as some random but determined power-hunters and self-projecting individuals obsessed with stealing from the state every second.

The Men of Goodies (MOGs)

The ruling class in Nigeria will not be complete without the businessmen in the sanctuary (BMS as I call them), who for the most part cleverly operate behind the curtains of both covert and overt politico-economic stage. These are supposedly men and women whose primary focus is the spiritual liberation and moral elevation of their followers or devotees.

Of course, preaching does not bake bread, but if the lives of these men and women are properly challenged and moulded by the honesty of both the preaching and the preacher, then grace finds a *template for moving men to bake the bread in response to the principle of the preaching.*

So the preachers don't have to be greedy lots. As preachers they are not to completely neglect the temporal needs of their people but that is not their primary assignment, if they lay proper and genuine spiritual and moral foundations for their people, their temporal needs will be taken care of by the authorities concerned who will be challenged by what they see and hear: the sound moral authority of the men of the sanctuary. After all, members of the ruling elites, are found in and among their flocks.

Unfortunately, only a few of those in the sanctuary are men of God. I have no apology for saying this. These hordes are called men of god, but, I think, perspicuously speaking, it will be more appropriate to call them by what they stand for *goodies,* and so I call them men of goodies. They are so-called because the services they offer the political class and all the public office 'mis-managers' who make up the nation's blind leadership college is a source of juicy patronage from those concerned, especially our largely sadistic and callous moneyticians.

These men of goodies do their job of protecting the politicians and affiliated money hawks with exceptional diligence and shrewdness by preaching messages that employ psycho-spiritual blind-folding tactics which force the people within their areas of influence to look elsewhere, unconsciously or involuntarily, while their economic-balls[10] are being fondled, by this means they neutralize the ocean-storms of their anger and possible revolts.

They give us the reasons why we must trust 'God' for our liberation, while at the same time we are tacitly encouraged or *psyched to neglect the indispensable roles proper to us in the schemes of obvious reality* for an illusory divine liberation.

They give us (we, the flocks) the bases for which we must obey our tormentors, oppressors and slave masters, even in the most *absurd circumstance*[11] that demands our immediate resistance as the oppressed. Instead of the pulpits[12] offering the harshest of condemnations of such absurd and unjust oppression and exploitation of the people, they go into Biblical silence mode. The shepherds of the flocks being attacked by the rapacious and ravenous wolves, in other words, the politicians, and their cohorts under the guise of (their detestable mantra) "the national interest", are *feeding their flocks with* sight blurring messages and feet-weakening admonition while ignoring the reality that smacks them in the face.

These Imams and Pastors; Priests and Prophets; Deacons and Bishops; Evangelists and Alfas *are agents of these ravenous wolves*, for the most part, they, from all indications, seem to discreetly work for these politicians and others who are somewhat considered to be in *the repulsive section of leadership class* in Nigeria. Thus, the men of goodies scratch the backs of these *prospective prison candidates living temporarily in palaces of gold and other precious stones built on the melting foundation of corruption* of varying degrees and the ill-fated stolen wealth; and these prospective prisoners scratch the backs of these men of goodies[13] in return with cool cash and other damned privileges –lands, cars, waivers etc.

However, for the fear that this perspective of mine might appear quite radical, rather than just a description of the reality we are often too quick to shy away from, let me just quickly poke your memory on one of the issues of the recent past.

For example, we all *saw* how one of these men of goodies, the former president of Christian

Association of Nigeria, Pastor Ayo Oritsejafor, a man who rose to national prominence through the instrumentality of CAN –Christian association of Nigeria, dramatized or exemplified this sickening collective moral leprosy of the pulpits right from the beginning of his tenure till the end of it, particularly from 2011 till 2015.

He stole nothing, not that we were told he didn't, but 'men of god' in *the alliance* don't steal, they simply collect the seeds from these thieves; after all, Psalm *24 vs 1 says the Lord is the earth and everything in it*. Sounds clear? Good. You got my point.

However, his chronic silence, like many other clerics, in the face of endemic thievery and arrogant corruption under the watchful eyes of his benefactor and fellow Niger-Deltan, president Goodluck Ebele Jonathan, was a grossly despicable *'public sin of complicity by deliberate silence'*. He remembered to pray for his reelection (of course, prayers are not a bad thing) and had a 'shrieking voice' to claim some people were trying to sabotage his (Jonathan's government), yet he never had even a childlike voice to condemn his government's endemic corruption.

In fact, his jet/plane was *used to ferry* millions of American dollar from Nigeria to South Africa[14] in 2014, the money was allegedly meant for the purchase of military *war toys* for the Nigerian Army. Of course, he came out to say that his jet was leased out by the company managing it on his behalf, thus he knew nothing about it. Wow! What a holy coincidence! Well, as the Yoruba will say: *oro oodun le'nu iya ole.* Literally meaning *mother of a known thief has got nothing sensible to say.*

Whether he, Pastor Ayo Oritsejafor (and his horde of sympathetic boot-licking pastors), knew anything about the Black Maria operation for which his jet was used or not, the fact that he has been fronting for a recklessly corrupt government led by a PhD wielding but clueless president, who almost skillfully run the ship of the state aground until the people threw him out of the ship's cabin, made a lot of us smell rat in the whole pedestrian drama of national shame, shown and talked about in the international public domain -television stations, newspapers and internet and radio.

The last general elections of March 28 (presidential and national assembly elections) and April 11 2015 (gubernatorial and state assembly elections) showed how grossly irresponsible and petty *the pulpits* can be when their hidden interests in the game of harvesting the *minds and bodies of those with the right keys to the treasuries of the state* (and its affiliated entities) for themselves and not for God are threatened.

Honestly, they, the pulpits with their annoyingly hypocritical stance on politicians and their sorrowfully puerile and distasteful public life, seem to be saying: "God? God is only concerned with their souls, is he not? So, he will get their souls at the appropriate time if he is lucky to ever have their erratic attention. But, for the time being, let us start with their pockets, bodies and minds first, after all, we will end up gaining their souls for him -God". They went all out against anyone who challenged their candidates' interests in retaining power or putting some puppets in office for various reasons that are only clear to these gatekeepers of hell and the associated miserable regions of the underworlds.

Verbal missiles, tactically covered with biblical threats, were fired across the battlefields of the 2015 general elections by these (pastors) *slaves of goodies* for our politicians. They saw all sorts of deception-inspired visions and gave profit-motivated prophecies (actually, mere monetized religious opinions) and assured them of coming out victorious. Can you imagine, even the wretched association of witches and wizards also came out to bite their piece of the cake of this general madness of constantly abusing religion and religious sentiments by saying they have chosen the would-be winners of 2015 elections. That was nothing but arrant nonsense!

Since certain ministers of religion have clients and they tried to protect their interests, I was surprised that the Emeres, Ogbanjes and Mamiwaters of Nigeria did not join the tacit but public support of politicians and their cohorts by many religionists. Have they lost their powers or they have never really had any to start with? Or they were just being careful? However, the season of cleric-political madness we experienced before, during and, to some extent, after 2015 general elections has shown us how deep-seated the errant-interests of the *pulpits* (i.e. the religious leaders) are in the ongoing unholy alliance between the sanctuary and government secretariats at the expense of the people of Nigeria.

From the South to the North and from the East to the West, this battle of shame raged on all through the pre-election days, weeks and months, and like wildfires in a waterless territory, it burnt everything on its way with ferocious stride.

In fact, Dr Goodluck, the president of the country at that point in time, being whom he was, calm, quiet and seemingly harmless but venomous, took full advantage of the tacit but misplaced supports of these men of goodies for him across the nation. I'm sure that you can think of one or two examples of your own without much effort.

Do you remember that shameful show of religious nonsense at Ota in Ogun state and at the Lagos-Ibadan Axis of religious deceptions and spiritual hocus-pocus? You remember, don't you? I guess you should, if you were alive enough to the happenings back then, then you should remember.

Only God knows how many cleric-political-king makers were covertly involved in the last general elections at all levels, but we heard how several of them overwhelmingly predicted victory for a host of incumbents at different layers of the government in Nigeria; all claiming to speak for their gods and goddesses or whatever name their irrational and unrealistic deities/demons bear.

Generally speaking, the people's voice, and of course, in addition to the over *miscalculation* of a billion-dollar-wielding Polithiefians Distributing Poverty (PDP) and the *restrained greed* of the Aggressive Power Changers (APC), ended up being the real voice of the True Rational Divine in the 2015 general elections.

So, our dear pastor goodie-goodies lost to an extent and the people, too, to another extent. To understand what I mean hear by both being losers of some sort, just look at the current national assembly members. In any case, the *restrained greedy ones* and the *apparently confused ones* are now ruling, at least they have some level of financial sanity more than the previous administration.

I have, however, noticed the growing sense of insecurity among the rich and the powerful, which is a good thing, if you asked me. They have realized that they are not really safe, irrespective of how many barrels of guns are employed for their protection. Their perimeter fences compete with those of Kuje prison in Abuja, and their so-called American barbed wires are stronger than the outer-bars of Kirikiri Maximum prison in Lagos.

You see? Congratulations to you all! They are closer to the real prison than the poor man on the street. Who can really feel safe in that sense with millions of empty stomachs, empty-heads and unoccupied hands all around them and their families? They know, too, nonetheless, that religion can and does neutralize anyone's malignant anger if those wielding religious influence over such people talk to them, especially those who have given their fate irrationally to religion.

I remember, during my undergraduate years, a prominent cleric once said, *those of you who say the clerics are doing nothing and religion is useless, at least, you should not deny that it saves your life from the people (poor's anger).* This truth is with us in this country. But how long that will work in favour of the exploitative elites? Consequently, bearing in mind the huge and often unquestioned influence of the religious leaders on the minds of the people they lead, the 'ruling gangs', I think, infer that they can really do business with religious leaders of the land, especially the heavyweight *goodie-goodie* clerics.

Hence, they pull every string that brings them in contact with these religious leaders, of course, the majority of these self-seeking men of the sanctuary long to have these politicians in and among their congregations, therefore they expect the string-pulling long before it was pulled by the politicians and their associates. However, in very rare circumstances, they actually *trick some of these men of the sanctuary who are genuine men of God -heart, body and soul,* by feigning complex piety and firm religiosity. Having won the friendship of groups of men of the sanctuary they launch irresistible handshake-processes that encourage the pulpits to stoutly stand for them too. Though not pointlessly in the open and not compulsorily in the backdoor meetings, but necessarily in the right atmosphere, the right arena and the right crowds -their congregations.

This friendship has brought the men of the sanctuary, economic-terrorists and political-billionaires together to form a powerful class that is very solid, influential and somewhat formidable. That is a class that determines the destinies of many; as though they are gods and goddesses or whatever deity people believe have such powers to alter their course in life.

When religion, money and crude Machiavellian[15] politics mix, what do we get? Empire of reckless rulers is what we get, no more no less[16]! Do not make the mistake of looking for the letter of alliance, you won't find one. It is not written. It is not official. It is only acted out and/or lived out. You can, however, find this *unwritten alliance* in the privileges granted, gifts given, the support offered and the courtesy visits exchanged. And also, you can see it in their *seemingly benign but exploitative and senselessly* quid quo pro pronouncements.

Believe it or not, if Nigeria will be better anytime soon, this fluid evil alliance must be broken from within and from without this class. How that will be achieved is not a question I set out to answer in this piece.

It is not the focus or the duty of this write-up to answer. Instead, the primary duty of this piece is to open the eyes of our minds to the fact of the existence of such (conscious or unconscious) formidable evil triad (or triangle of evil) that enslaves this nation and impedes its progress by enhancing its stagnation. If you ask more questions from those who govern you and look more intently at their actions and inactions, you might be the first to liberate many.

The real political party members are united by their similar broad aspirations and collectively adopted well-defined ideology, and thus they motivate and rally the voters and the general sentiments of the populace in support of (and on behalf of) the defined targets and goals of the group.

Chapter 15

ERRORS OF POLITICAL PARTIES IN NIGERIA

A political party is an affairs-of-the-state oriented organization within a country that brings people who share the same broad system of social beliefs, political outlooks and aspirations or ambitions for governing together. It does this by presenting or attempting to present its members for election to governmental positions through which it achieves its grand *ideology*[1] or well-defined socio-political outlooks and ambitions.

Thus members of a real political party are united by their similar broad aspirations and collectively adopted well-defined ideology, and so they motivate and rally the voters and the general sentiments of the populace in support of and on behalf of the defined targets and goals of the group (i.e. the party).

For the most part, in many of the countries (that are) truly open to the democratic culture of allowing and promoting genuine participation of their citizens in the elective processes (or business of governance), the political parties play vital functions in the overall democratic evolution and/or progression. These parties put together political ideology (or normative beliefs) and policy direction, select candidates through party primaries/valid selection processes, sponsor or support electioneering campaigns for their candidates, and scrutinize the work of the members elected to governmental positions for the overall good of the nation and strategic interest of the party.

Political parties provide the appropriate or necessary connections between the governed and the government, by opening up channels for the citizens to make their minds known to their government in a clear-cut manner, especially through their votes or elected representatives.

Having pointed out what political parties are and their most fundamental duties, I turn my attention right away to some easily discernible fundamental problems of political associations in Nigeria which we loosely call parties, and these errors (i.e. problems) can be summed up as follow:

- ✓ Lack of a predefined group ideology
- ✓ A conglomeration of undesirable elements

The Lack of Pre-defined Group Ideology

First, our political associations, or political parties as we either lavishly or erroneously call them, are fundamentally defective. Thus their flawed structure affects their mode of existence and, in the long run, their functions or their socio-political and economic efficiency for the overall good of the nation. Nigeria political parties, for the most realistic part, have next to no ideologies (well-organized normative values and beliefs). And the *concrete absence of this very important conceptual foundation is the number one error of political parties* in Nigeria. Put plainly, as it stands Nigeria's political parties are without discernible, concrete, clear-cut, *hardwired*[2] or specific ideology or socio-economic and politico-cultural values, beliefs and objectives that should, as a matter of necessity, form the root of their policy thrust.

I challenge you, the reader, to do a sincere research on the most realistically known standard or understanding or function(s) of political parties in some real or even in some pseudo-democratic environments across the world and you will be amazed that our political parties, if they may be so called, are, to a great extent, malfunctioning or defective or technically non-existent because they lack necessary ideological (or normative) spirit.

Although they generate empty slogans almost every day and fill our ballot papers with shallow symbols[3] that have little or no connection with the immediate or remote reality of *problem identification and solution generation.*

A conglomeration of Undesirable Elements

The second point, the effects of the foundational error: since our parties lack organized, rational and realistic socio-political logic, it means the political house built on such foundation is nothing but a death trap. Therefore, what this lack of clear-cut political and socio-economic belief system causes a *chaotic amalgam of confused conservatives, opportunistic liberals, theory-laden socialists, hardcore or pathological political businessmen and other undesirable political elements.*

That is the second error of political parties/associations in Nigeria; and this is why Nigeria political parties are largely a congregation of predatory political birds, hyenas, wolves, attack dogs, scorpions, black mambas, tortoises and; perhaps, some doves and lambs on the edge of the congregating lot.

Since there is no rationally discernible radical basis for their coming together to form a political association, and bearing in mind the fact of their *actual disordered* existence as a group, they implicitly adopt sophists' principle of *might is right* and those within the association equipped with more aggressive animal instincts drag the association along the same politically moribund, economically disruptive and ever maliciously-winding and tumultuous paths they tread individually.

Permit me to briefly take a more critical look at the two connected points I raised above within the template of an observed reality in this my beloved Nigeria.

Lack of Predefined Political Logic (Revisited)

Just as I have stated above, Nigeria's political associations are only lavishly or erroneously called *parties, but in reality,* they are fundamentally defective and structurally flawed associations. When a group of people come together on the basis of cosmetic and superficial group policy they can only thrive in a pattern that makes them look healthy as a group for a while and the ills of such faulty union will only, as matter of necessity, emerge as they progress in their collective journey of *colourful charades and mutual deceptions.*

Having a defined template of operation in any endeavour in life helps one to carefully watch the steps we, as human beings, take so that one avoids veering off the right track of progress. In addition, it makes it easy for us to know those people and things that might not fit into the dream we have; those who might be obstructive or hostile to the *vision* into which we have translated our *dream;* and those whose presence might be subversive to the *mission* we have mapped out for attaining *the vision* eventually, all things being equal.

Thus, in the case of political parties, a *logically realistic, organized and holistic socio-political system of beliefs, values, and ideas forming the basis of a social, economic, or political philosophy* of a party is very, very important or indispensable for a genuine progressive democratic evolution and economic advancement of a nation. I mean a seriously responsible nation desirous of multi-dimensional growth and development within the shortest time possible, will adopt a logically realistic ideology-based party system in its democratic culture instead of the disjointed snap-thought based associations we have around. Even as old as People Democratic Party is, it is still a shameful example of disjointed snap-thought based organization and All Progressive Congress is not less guilty either.

A party's political ideology here is not the same as our weird 'sloganistic' orientation which glories in the mere 'deification' of empty catchphrases, mottos, tags and watchwords on Ankara, *Aso-ebi,* party buses, branded T-shirts, wristbands etc. No, it goes beyond that! It goes beyond '*APC … Change!'* slogans or '*PDP … Power to the people'* mantras which rented the very air we breathed before, during and immediately after the last general elections (2015 presidential and state elections); and are renting the air again in preparation for 2019 elections.

We are very good at preparing for elections and not governance, and that's a big problem with/for us –our politicians especially. We, politically speaking, are like expert exam-takers but not students of applied knowledge; after the exams, such students know little or next to nothing or remember nothing from all they memorized and wrote in the examinations, notwithstanding their seemingly near-perfect performance in examinations.

Political ideology is more coherent, more rational and more connected to the real socio-economic values than mere attractive but empty catchphrases. Though ideology might be, somewhat, reasonably put in part in catchphrases, it cannot be exhausted by catchphrases or empty slogans. The moment it does, that very moment it (the ideology) dies. And, mind you, the ideology must be meticulously conceived and tactically and realistically developed before coining out catchphrases from it and not the other way round.

Unfortunately, however, here in Nigeria, like in many other countries that are suffering from leadership haemorrhages and ideological drought, catchphrases are thoughtlessly generated and recklessly woven into beautiful verbal garments of illusions and confusing pictures of paralyzed figments-of-the-imagination.

However, in our pathetic political context, people carve out party slogans and afterwards, those responsible for their (slogans) generation start asking themselves what those catchphrases or slogans in question are actually meant to convey to everyone - both the people outside their political walls and to those within the walls themselves. What a colony of blind navigators!

It is a fact of life that moving at high *speed in an expensive custom-made automobile on a completely wrong road (or direction) with the most experienced driver* behind the wheel will never take you to the right destination. Except, of course, you realize the fact that you are not on the right road (or direction), turn back and start re-navigating your way to and through the right road (direction).

I remember a joke that was told about a (federal) minister who campaigned for the re-election bid of a politically pathetic former Nigerian president.

It was (the joke) said that when the minister went to campaign in one of the very poor towns within his home state, he said so many things about what his party planned to do for them, and promised that the president will give power to the people by taking it from some cabals who did not want life to be nice and smooth -selenkejoo[4]- for them.

Two days after they, the minister and his team, left the poor state where they had campaigned and returned to his cozy palace-like abode in Abuja, one of his most trusted aides summoned courage to go to his office during office hours and asked him how the gift of power to the people was to be achieved, judging from the way things have been for years under their party's rule, and worst still, the state of affairs at that point in time in 2015.

"Oga sir, well done" the aide greeted on entering the minister's office, the minister who spread himself in his seat like Olumo-rock[5], looked at the aide and said:

"Yes, thank you Kabir" replied the minister dismissively

"Please I have a question and it is about what you said on the campaign ground and what our great party has been mouthing for..."

"Mallam Kabir to the point..." cuts in the minister impatiently

"Sorry sir" the aide apologized

"Just the point Mallam or Kabir" snapped the minister

"Okay, sir. How exactly do we intend to give power to the people?" The aide asked, with his hand folded behind his back as if he was before a tyrant king.

"We?" the minister snapped, his eyeballs betrayed a mixture of confusion and embarrassment.

"Sorry sir, I meant to say you," the aide said calmly

"Me? Are you out of your mind?" the minister said angrily while rising to his feet, the aide took three cautious steps backwards.

"Sorry Sir," said the aide

"Keep your apology! Look I am not the one you should be asking this 'power to the people' thing" said the minister, who seemed more embarrassed than angry with his own response to his aide question.

"Ask the party chairman or members of the board of trustee or ask him, I mean Mr President himself," he said as he

pointed his index finger at the picture of the president on the wall of his office.

"I only said what we have been saying for the past sixteen years and what, I think, the people always want to hear. Don't they? What they mean by that is not clear to me myself. All I know is that it brings me meal tickets. Who are the people? What power are we talking about and who will give the power to the people?" the minister said rhetorically

The aide's eyes squinted and his head bent leftward, his left forearm rested on his back a little above his backside, his right hand raised halfway between his shoulder and waist with the index finger jutting out of the camp of folded fingers. A clear gesture of "I...have.....questions...." common to non-confident pupils in primary school. But the minister was not ready for more bombardment; he may not survive it if he allowed it.

"Mallam Kabir, don't look at me like that, drop your hand" , the minister ordered.

"This is not a classroom, this is an office of the government of the federal republic and, no more questions, please! I did not bring you here to be questioning me; did I? Are you working for the oppositions now? Enh? But in all sincerity I don't know how they will do it, and I don't care. That is if

ever there was an intention to do anything like that. But we, the politicians and our foot soldiers, can pretend to be the people while the party acts as the one giving us the power! Am sure that makes some sense" the minister said rapidly and flatly with certain callousness in his tone, then, he walked out of his office, leaving the poor aide more confused than he was before asking the question.

The above joke portrays, to a great extent, the general picture of the degenerated orientation of political parties when looking at party ideology in the context of *our* Nigerian 21st-century politics of slogans.

Those who should drive the ideological train of party politics are not even sure of what to think of or how to think it out logically, that is if there is anyone honest and capable of doing it among them. How will a clueless party leader direct the process of a party's ideological formulation?

Consequently, there seems to be no concern or no genuine interest among a large chunk of party politicians for such a psycho-intellectual infrastructure which can and does help in getting steady attainment of set goals, and when set goals are attained it helps in providing a certain degree of pre-configured template for maintaining the successes achieved. However, in case of unanticipated failures, it aids in mitigating the debilitating effects of such failures; failures which at any rate will come one way or the other, anticipated or not.

Lacking this all-important rational conceptual model, called political ideology, makes such a political party or political organization a mere drifting body of syncretic politically-intelligent simpletons[6], who will, sooner or later, drown the immediate future of those they lead or mortgage it carelessly or carefully. In the Yoruba language (of western Nigeria) such a group without ideological spine will simply be termed *Egbe Iruwa-Ogiriwa*[7].

Our collective political experience as a country is filled with the repulsive images and voices of the abominable college of ideologically dead or moribund political organizations. Politicians, at least let us give them this titular privilege though the majority of them do not deserve to be so called, criss-cross political enclaves in Nigeria with nauseating, disgusting, and detestable carelessness.

They give almost the same indefensible excuse whenever they politically fornicate about in their primitive village of nude politics without any ideological harmony: *"I left party BDB because my people wanted me to leave"* or *"we joined party ABC because the interests of my people were at risk"*.

Imagine! Can you see what emptiness can do to its hosts? How empty are our politicians and the parties that throw many of them up for elective positions?

Who are the people they keep referring to as *my people?* I wonder. Perhaps the people are their Jezebel-like wives, their vile children and a host of boot-liking damned creatures nastily called supporters who care less about the development of our collective society.

Well, this is Nigeria you may be surprised to know that there are some educated-hand-outs among those whom they refer to as 'my people', as though they were their possessions.

If the political parties were thoroughly driven by ideology or some degree of rational politics, an adult who is mentally stable[8] and is drilled in the principles of such party before or after joining such party, and still goes ahead to stay within such a party based on his acceptance of what such party stands for and hopes to achieve, will not find it easy jumping from one party to the other at every moment of *collective political discomfort,* or his personal electoral misfortune within such a party.

No, ideologically educated and disciplined politicians will not be jumping, every now and then, from party A to B, as though he is a joyous but wild, primitive and thoughtless gorilla that jumps from one tree to another in celebration of his irrational and lower jungle freedom which , unfortunately, is caged by massive *prison of animal-level* intelligence.

A conglomeration of Undesirable Elements Inspired By War-Booty Mindset

Flowing from the points I made in the paragraphs above, the absence of ideological foundation leads necessarily to the conglomeration of undesirable political elements. People whose sole inspiration for coming into a political party or, for forming one is neither for the growth of the party and its structure nor the development of the socio-political entity –the country- they live or subsist in. Instead, these people join the party or come together with the sole aim of using the party as [a] mere battleship for conquering political wars, and, not just winning elective positions of authority in the government of the state and its affiliated agencies.

Their concern is not the growth of the state as a living entity or to achieve the vision of the party for the state's democratic growth, techno-economical development and socio-cultural advancement. No, they can't see beyond their noses, that is if, ideology-wise, they see at all.

Do you blame them? No, don't blame people (who are) accustomed to retrogressive socio-political thought pattern and people who, by design, choose to become members of political parties that run their own very existence like the body of a soul-less, aimless and directionless crowd that has an indeterminate destination.

When a political organization does not have properly defined *standard of operation and realistic goals for the collective good of the nation,* it becomes a den for sycophants, opportunists and political robbers. If a *political organization is not positively-discriminatory*[9] about its core political value system, or its principles of admitting only those who utterly accept its ideological standpoints, the natural result is that such a party becomes attractive, very attractive to anyone with emotional muscles for a war-like relationship.

They develop stomachs for Machiavellian scheming and, tongues designed and forged in the depth of hell for poisoning society. Their smiles are seemingly honest but more deceitful than the ancient Eveline-serpent[10], ruthless national progress killers with a false sense of invincibility.

Our own Nigerian democratic experience in the last 19 years, like in other pseudo-democratic environments of the world, is full of images of the political and socio-economic failures occasioned by ideologically disordered political parties and politicians lacking collective direction and individual discipline.

Thus, since nature abhors a vacuum, that means people cannot come together for *nothing,* something must bring them together, no matter how indiscernible or negligible it might seem. Consequent upon this fact, the invisible glue that holds politicians together in (norm-less or) ideology-less Nigerian political parties is the actual but unwritten and unspoken rule of *chop-make-I-chop or share-the-loot or come-and-chops.*

Put plainly, the hope of sharing political 'war-booty'[11] is a powerful force that brings them hurriedly and aggressively together like soldiers of fortune in one political battleship, referred to as a party.

For example, the manner the former ruling party at the federal level -PDP, and its members came to power since 1999 and sustained themselves in power for uninterrupted four-terms (16 years), was and is a good image of thoughtless association that possesses everything but ideology-based direction.

They had no value-oriented and norms-guided interactions; it was all about power for the sake of power. It was a grossly deplorable relationship.

The central glue was the principle of *come-and-chop,* and this *come-and chop* principle was a good bait that brought more foxes to the hole but 'could' not create the necessary orderliness needed for conquering more territories. Then, a more ruthless person or persons with more aggressive animal instincts have to act as the power-balancing agents or direction determining navigators, irrespective of their disordered socio-political logic.

Bear in mind that no matter how perilous the path they choose may be, everyone interested in the anticipated loot will be drawn or attracted to them.

Please, do a little research on the party that ruled from 1999 to 2015 with special emphasis on 1999-2007 and 2011-2015, then you see how a party can really be a congregation of the war-booty minded people? Of course, since the party is not a complete replica of hell, you will find some doves among them but, unfortunately, they are usually on the periphery.

Besides, another example of the high-definition effect (HDE) of not having strong conceptual political-cum-ethical cut-out or ideology or rational standard of operation by which every intending member must abide is what is currently happening to APC the new ruling party at the centre (of the Federal Republic) of Nigeria. Though core party supporters, members and sympathizers may disagree with me, their disagreement does not matter, what matters is whether what *I have to say is a good shot at the target of reality.*

Before APC was formed on February 6, 2013, and eventually registered by INEC on July 31st of the same year, different independent political forces who wanted a share of PDP's political fortunes were coalescing.

Some forces were fighting for space to exist as a political entity. Some were fighting for proper recognition within their (own) political enclave; while some were mere noisemakers and attention-seekers who actually did not even know what they wanted or how to get what they wanted. Still, (some) others were already on their feet walking on the path of developing an image of the ideology-based party but were having problems with their lower selves –greed for power.

And yet, there was also a particular tiny group comprising men of integrity that seemed more focused and organized but were, somewhat, economically insignificant; and there were others who were only looking for any space that could ensure that they lived decently on state financial blood, even if it was infected with the curses of the masses.

In short, different groups and individuals wished they were the ones ruling (or ruining) the *Nigerian state* then, even though they (or a chunk of the polithiefians) were not *equipped for the lowest form of leadership let alone at the highest level.*

So, eventually, they came together to form a political party called APC based on their common desire to capture the power and share the loot. In fairness to them, a (tiny) few of them wanted to advance the good of the people as well – e.g. the Bakare and Buhari axis of the defunct CPC and others.

Yes, the beginning of the story has the seed of its end in it; they captured power at the centre or won the presidential election if you prefer that. Then problems started brewing, perhaps earlier than the majority of them had expected. Although many of us saw it coming, and in fact, we did not just see it coming, we have observed that their lack of clear-cut template or ideology to which *everyone must subscribe* to before being given a place in their political denomination or colony, was in itself a fertile ground for discord. And if proper steps were not taken, it could be a possible seed of implosion. Well, I am not saying the party will implode now, but it can still implode any time soon.

What I am saying, in essence, is that we need to understand that a political party is an important institution within the whole 'democratic complex' itself, since it supports the stability of political culture, electoral (voter) education and ideals, thereby strengthening the progression of democratic processes of a country or a nation.

Hence, conglomerating undesirable elements inspired by war-booty mindset alone; or creating a specialized pool of confused and clueless individuals whose governing propensity is to amass wealth (and power), irrespective of the dire national need for political growth and economic development, in the name of political parties is nothing but a basis for perpetuating those errors. Those errors have helped our political parties to impart everything on their members except politically pragmatic knowledge and art of state management.

In the final analysis, for any political association to be able to graduate, from mere *union of people propelled by their debased hunger for power for the sake of accumulating wealth,* to a desirable political party that, first and foremost, seeks the advancement of common good of Nigerians (and our the nation) and the solidification of developmental political culture, it must re-examine the basis of its existence and redefine its objectives, socio-political value-system and group discipline.

Unfortunately, those concerned in this political tragedy of parties without any semblance of norms and values (ideology), group discipline and discernible socio-political value-system etc., are *too immersed in their pathetic desire to create empires by manipulating their political colonies called parties* –from Lagos to Adamawa, Ogun to Kano, Imo to Akwa-Ibom and so on.

These are almost always the same indigenous colonizers with little interest of the colonies at heart. These errors of political parties in Nigeria will continue, as long they are not tackled headlong by those who should do the tackling.

Somebody must, as a matter of necessity, think outside our rotten political box, Nigerians deserve a better political system. Yes, we do.

Living and existing will be crushingly boring if we are all (wo)men and we all dress the same way and speak one language and so on.

Chapter 16

ETHNO-CENTRIC PEDESTRIANISM OF THE ELITES

'Ethnicity' is ordinarily one of the beauties (or colours) of the human society; if it is understood for what it was inherently designed for by the creator of man, which is, *to be the spice of life, not the spite of life.*

Ethnicity (socio-cultural variety) is a universal phenomenon that when seen as it should genuinely be, then, we shall value how it gives meaning to our understanding of variety, diversity and difference.

For instance, loosely speaking, in the animal world we see 'ethnicity' in its lowest form possible. Lion and tiger are said to be members of cat the family, yet they are not cats. This variety brings beauty to our understanding and appreciation of the wildlife, and we are ready to do everything possible *to preserve these different species of animals* in their natural habitat.

Nonetheless, we are eager and willing to allow our animal-level instinct to rule us when dealing with our fellow men and women, who, by no choice or fault of theirs, were born into different human languages and socio-cultural traditions, called ethnics or tribes or races.

The sad news about our lives as human beings, and most especially as Nigerians, is that the higher many of us go in our intellectual, political and financial capacity, the more ethnocentric and debased we actually become. In fact, things like the academic gown; the turban; the Roman-collar; the 'legislative sceptre' and 'the Naira' that should, ordinarily, represent higher human values are now turned into *empty symbols of decadence in the path of societal development.*

Of course, one would expect that people who are politically 'non-relevant', with low intellectual achievement and high financial aridity or nothingness will be the actual peddlers of vain-glorious ethnocentric pedestrianism or the projectors of blindfolded tribal superiority, but that is not the reality.

The reality, unfortunately, is that the worst peddlers of perverted understanding of the beauty of our differences are the so-called elites; the academic, political, religious, and the financial every-weight[1].

They lay more emphasis on what divides the people who have lived peacefully together for years with little or no crisis; instead of emphasizing the greater things that unite them, that is, *their common humanity, and their collective/individual desire to have a peaceful and meaningful life,* not just to exist on the edge of life.

Thus, they whip up ethnoreligious sentiments, not necessarily because they love their people more than anyone else, but because they want to milk them without their knowledge. Or at least delay the people's knowledge about such an act of *subtle but immensely malicious manipulation* being carried out on their lives by the elites, the so-called leaders.

I wonder *what is wrong with being an Ibo man with his full cultural consciousness as long as he respects* the cultural consciousness of other people with different socio-cultural backgrounds.

I can't still believe that in this 21st century Nigeria, many of the miserable elites of various *colours and shades* still ethnicize every aspect of our national and 'minor local' life; even for the most minute of issues that has nothing to do with the origin of any group whatsoever in this country. It is pathetic, and shame on you fools!

The miserable and abominable lots, generally called the elites, are so pedestrian in their approach to issues of national importance that they *twist and weave* every situation that does not favour them and their accursed households around the texture of their ethno-cultural and religious orientations. Even when in the most average world of reasoning, there is no connection between the two ends they are trying to draw a line of (un)necessary connection. It is very pathetic to have political, academic, religious and financial classes that seem irredeemably pedestrian, petty and puerile, but also malevolent in the way they exploit the sensitive and explosive nature of ethnoreligious sentiments of a population suffering from *crushing multi-dimensional* poverty.

We, the ordinary people of Nigeria, care less about where you come from; we welcome you more readily when we know you are a stranger in our midst. We are amazing when it comes to loving strangers, whether he's from the East, or West, or North, or South. I know this because I have been in those corners of the winds.

All that kindness, however, is being poisoned and threatened with extinction, by our readiness to irrationally fight the battles of these evil elites, especially the polithiefians, who feed fat on our divisions. We can't be their slaves, we are Nigerians, and we must assert our freedom to an inter-cultural and inter-religious rational association.

Don't get me wrong, there is nothing wrong in talking about one's ethnicity in a manner that enhances solidarity for the good of such an ethnic group and strengthens the bond of brotherhood among them. While in the long run, it initiates and nourishes bonds with other groups across the imaginary ethnic boundaries within one, peaceful and progressive Nigeria.

Everything, however, is wrong with it, if the solidarity among any group will be fortified through the campaign of hatred against the well-being of every other group outside (y)our chaotic tribal worldviews!

Those who should know better have miserably decided to know little, if they actually know anything at all about the huge benefits of inter-cultural mutual respect and co-responsibility, and since they know little, they and their worldviews cannot but be repulsively little.

The saddest thing about these ethnocentric division-peddlers is that many of them, I mean these 'glorious-fools', just like their counterparts in advanced the nations, too, are professors and PhD holders; pastors and imams; priests and bishop; many are senators, governors and ex-governors; ministers and ex-ministers and ex-heads of state; many are bankers and financial experts; business moguls, the list of these *dis-honourables* is almost endless.

These are people that can be said to have seen and have conquered in their various fields of endeavours, but they are a bunch of enslaved big-things-in-little-things. In plain English, they are *big for nothing!* You people are bloody cowards. You find strength and joy in the division of peace-loving Nigerians.

Ethnicity is all about sharing distinctive cultural traits as a group in society. In other words, it is a kind large family with common socio-cultural heritage. And nature has more hand in the creation or evolution of this large family than individuals making up the group. Anthropologically speaking, we can explain how humankind evolves in all its aspects, especially human culture and its development. And in the sociological context, we can dig into the origin, development, and structure of human societies and behaviour of individual groups and people in the society.

We, however, cannot stop the existence of different cultural groups in the larger society; they will always be there in different forms. In its broadest sense, ethnicity, I make bold to say, is an indispensable constituent element of the universe because there are several millions of different levels of realities that give meaning to our world and; and in the strictest sense of the word, ethnicity gives meaning to human society in a way nothing else can (replace).

I think socio-cultural variety or ethnicity is designed to be part of human universal consciousness from day one by the creator of the world. Sincerely speaking, I am of the view that living and existing would have been crushingly boring if we are all (wo)men and we all dress the same way and speak one language and so on.

Looking below the surface, therefore, I acknowledge that the champions of mischievous interpretation of socio-cultural differences, in whatever name it is called –racism for the USA and other advanced economies, tribalism for Africans, and ethnicism for the rest of the world etc., - are all over the globe. Yet, I still maintain that here in Nigeria it is worse than we think.

It evolves in a manner that makes it elude the radars of objective consciousness of majority of the population because the elites have helped it to develop a unique but malevolent *biostealthsomatic*[2] existence; in other words, they have successfully remade exploitative-ethnicity in 'detection proof image', so that it exists in a cunning manner that hides its dangerous presence from people's consciousness.

That's why your wife, for example, will unconsciously remember you are a Hausa man when she wants to talk about everything bad, yet she won't see anything wrong with every evil of her Yoruba kin's men and women. It is that bad.

They are so efficient with their new found *ethno-nanopsychology*[3] of biostealthsomatic existence to the extent that even the most detribalized section of their ethnic groups blindly become the foot soldiers of these selfish and power-hungry slaves of opportunity called elites.

These slaves of opportunity are becoming more successful with their ill-willed desire to bring their ethnic groups to power using every-and-any means possible. Like 'Adolf Hitler', they psyche people into believing that they are unique race and so deserve the best, deserve to rule, and deserve to have a place of pride in the scheme of things always. Even when it is obvious that they have nothing to prove it, they still shout it repeatedly to themselves, until it becomes an ethnic lyric and a tribal dogma.

Their actual desire, however, is to grab the power of the state for themselves and their vile offspring. They are only using the ever-sensitive ethnoreligious sentiments as the *aviation fuel* for their damned flight to the high mountains of presidential, gubernatorial, senatorial or ministerial *thrones of hell.* Though blood may flow on the street in the process of their damned ascent to the bloody thrones, they don't care, at least not about us the real people of Nigeria. Why should they care anyway, when none of their children is involved?

For these elites, the people are seen as nothing but 'the fuel' needed for the journey to their desired political destinations. In other words, the fuel is used (I mean burnt) to produce the necessary driving force for their 'vehicle's engine'; which means the people are never the object of their desires, power is. So they –the masses- are not the end in themselves, but are a means to an end for this *elitist brood of vipers*[4].

Hence, the fuel is useful only to the extent to which it enables the engines to generate the much-needed propelling power for the whole body mass of the vehicle (i.e. the elites' ambitions). Regrettably, however, as they progressively ruin our dreams of a simple but meaningful life in this country, their own families are among the passengers on board, enjoying the cozy custom-made 'executive plane of juicy offices', while we, who play the foolish ethnic foot soldiers, are used as the aviation fuel. It's a metaphor, just think.

Their *pedestrian ethnic definition* of everything that goes against their ambitions is more demonic and vicious than a legion of those 'innocent demons' they chase around in their religious houses every day. It is more lunatic and harebrained than the hordes of animals-in-human-skins called Boko-haram, our home-grown terrorists that ravaged and wreaked havoc on north-east Nigeria.

Their ethnoreligious pettiness is more irrational and self-destructive than the activities of *Niger Delta Avengers* and other insane criminals and saboteur in the cloak of militancy in the South-south. It is more primitive and backward than the activities of killer-herdsmen (Fulani or not) all over Nigeria.

This pedestrian ethnicism is more regressive, greedy and abominable than the kidnapping industry initially dominant in the south-east and now everywhere in Nigeria. And finally, but not exhaustively, I dare say here that the pedestrian ethnocentrism of the elites anywhere is *more of high-treason* than the looting of our commonwealth is.

Their definition of ethnicity is ruining our life as a nation. The latent inter-ethnic mutual suspicion has been excavated by the elites, and now it reigns supreme in the sub-consciousness of millions. For how long do we have to be ruled by this nonsense?

Well, the answer I have not, but as long as political offices or positions are involved, I encourage you to try to listen to the most basic conversations of most Nigerians on the street and behind *laced-curtains* of big offices, and you shall always feel the texture of the covert taste of mutual ethnic-suspicion.

Therefore, unless, we, the people resist the increasing biostealthsomatic ethnicization of our collective consciousness, it may become our normalized way of thinking, relating and interacting, in which case, we would have lost our freedom as people for life to our divide and rule maestros.

The religious 'circle' should be the most immune to evils of exploitative ethnicity, yet it is among the most 'open circles' to such evils. This is not mere speculation it is a fact, and I speak from experience, too.

These religious leaders tacitly support ethno-centric biases and tactically cover them up under various senseless guises of supporting the truth, instilling discipline and engendering justice, but what they do is actually the opposite of what they claim.

For instance, how many of the higher-up clerics from the Yoruba, Ibo, Hausa, Urhobo, Tiv, Kanuri, Itsekiri etc., extractions would allow *qualified* clerics from other tribal extractions to take up sensitive positions of authority within their 'nativized' religious hierarchy at the expense of their *unqualified* tribesmen?

I will not waste time asking the same question about actors in the political, financial, academic and social circles in this country. Let me, categorically, state here that the elites always want to perpetuate themselves in power at all cost, and one of the major ways to do that in this country without *khaki and boot*s is to mix our religious and tribal sentiments in a shrewd but explosive manner. A kind of gunpowder and matchbox politics, call it Manipulation 101, and you would be right.

Politicians have been the most prominent beneficiaries of exploitative-ethnicity, but politics is the worst victim of its evils. Of course, every aspect of Nigeria is being ruined daily; education and religion are not excluded. Ethno-centric pedestrianism of the elites has shown over and over again, that education without proper human integration or formation is a cherished waste of time.

I believe education is for integrated knowledge, so knowledge for proper human self-integration and freedom of the mind must be evolved more aggressively in Nigeria now, more than ever before. This will go a long way in opening the eyes of the mind of many of us to see the myriad of ways those ethnoreligious and socio-political issues we care so much about are, dishonestly, used by the elites, across the board, to manipulate us for their selfish interest at the detriment of the rest of us.

Remember, these elites have told us over and over again that God will help us. Yet, they help themselves to lucrative positions and pull their kinsmen and women along.

So my question is: why can't God help us in sharing such positions?

Instead of God sharing these positions, they forcibly keep them in their political pockets, while at the same time they try to wrestle for more positions at any expense, including spilling our innocent blood. If hell is real, then the hottest part of it is your resting place, *oh you heartless vipers!*

They claimed zoning will solve the problem of tribal grievances, but it has helped to reinforce the concept of *we against them;* a shortcut to the tragedy of it is *our mediocre turn.* When zoning, in my honest observation, is actually a game of divide and rule as appropriate.

Zoning is an advanced weapon for destroying collective tranquillity, team engineering and unity. It is a holy poison that the pedestrian and lazy-head politicians and their associates in other fields developed to turn people against each other while pretending it is a tool for socio-political justice. If, for instance, we zone based on the 6 geopolitical zones and over 250 ethnic groups, do you think the wheels of inter-ethnic and interreligious cohesion will ever revolve on their axes? Holy nonsense! What a scientific deception!

It has reinforced division among our people more than it actually gives any socio-political justice. Our zoning fluke is like saying Barack Obama must be American president in order to evolve a just society and improve the state of his 'skins-men', but his eight years in office has not changed the degrading treatment of his 'skins-men'[5]. Why?

Because he is but one man, his skins-men need to get more politically involved and stop nit-picking in their homes. So, zoning in our national life has strengthened the tyranny of mediocrity instead of establishing the supremacy of meritocracy. Zoning is a form of political hand-out that reinforces strategic political impotency and encourages a false sense of 'waiting for our turn' or an illusory sense of political sportsmanship.

It has relegated the progressive team-spirit to the background and hoisted the flag of jaundiced individualism. It has resurrected the (*sicut) cadaver* of '*if it is not of us, then it is not for us*' mindset. And, my friend, that is a disaster and a shame.

Question: can any geopolitical zone or region in Nigeria become dominant political force without the support of at least two of the other geopolitical zones? The answer is emphatic, no. So we need more of team engineering that strengthens unity other than this *polithiefical* zoning madness.

Wait a minute! Am I outrightly condemning the soul of zoning? No, but I am calling your attention to the visible sicknesses of the ethnocentric-pedestrianism of those we entrust our common dreams into their unworthy hands in the name of zoning.

Put differently, I am, without reservation, condemning those who hijack the control of our common dreams and coat it with their own version of sugary poison they call zoning. These pedestrian-ethnicists will stoke the fire of particular political concepts wrapped in the outwardly beautiful but inwardly rotten idea of the right of their people, only when they are not favoured by a particular socio-economic regime.

However, when they snake their way to the corridors of power, then the concept will assume a different colouration. Hence the people are used as mere tools for war; they are means to an end and not the end in themselves –the masses are to them the dispensable-disposables.

Restructuring, for instance, was one of the most 'classic songs' of our power politics, if not the most 'classical song', in the modern-ancient[6] political opera of Nigeria.

But what happens when those political opera-conductors come to power? The same celebrated piece of political music becomes un-performable and unfit for the political opera any more. Nonsense! Why is the APC dominated government not restructuring Nigeria? Because to them, like the dying PDP, a government is just and patriotic when it is doing their bidding, whether tacitly or openly. And a government is unfair, tribal, sectional and unpatriotic when they are left out of the so-called juicy political positions.

For example, the Jonathanian government (2010- May 29 2015) was for many of these pedestrian-elites in one camp, especially those from the east and north of the Niger, the fairest and most patriotic government in the history of Nigeria. However, 'political left-outs' in other parties, however, especially those from the West of the Niger, claimed that Jonathanian government was the most calmly dangerous and anti-western region when talking about the distribution of *juicy government positions*. You see, it is all about the elites.

Of course, not all elites fall into these two broad categories during that administration, because some in the administration still found excuses to grind axe with it, not because they love their people so well but largely because they didn't get the opportunity to taste what other supporters suck from the *marrow* of our dear nation's dying economy.

Now, President Muhammadu Buhari assumed office on May 29 2015, and he is now the dartboard of both genuine agitator-elites and pedestrian-elites. The pedestrian elites in the west are having their muted fair share of the ministerial positions, and yet they would have preferred to have more.

In the south-east and south-south, these elites are weeping privately for lost opportunities, but in public, they are presenting their pains in the cloak of the pains of their people. So they shout 'South-east, the indigbo are being marginalized! 'Yeyh, hey ! The Hausa-Fulani have filled every available position in government with their tribesmen'. 'Oh the Niger Delta is being punished for whatever', they cry.

But who among these unfortunate vipers does not know the fact that the whole northern Nigeria cannot and must not be lumped, under any condition, into an only Muslim-Hausa-Fulani umbrella? That would be a cruel injustice. Don't they know how huge the number of non-Hausa ethnic groups in the Middle-belt (north central) and the north-east are?

There are three regions in the north of Nigeria, and Hausa-Fulani life's fluid does not flow in everyone's blood. Although the Hausa language is commonly spoken by many people living in the north, it does not mean they are all of Hausa or Fulani extraction.

For instance, the North-west comprises of Kaduna, Kano, Katsina, Jigawa, Kebi, Zanfara and Sokoto states. Northcentral includes Plateau, Nassarawa, Benue, Niger, Kwara and Kogi states. And the north-east states of Borno, Gombe, Taraba, Adamawa, Yobe and Bauchi. Those from the north-central area are anything but Hausa-Fulani.

Hence, if this president chooses one person from each state of the north, the north will still have more people in those ministerial positions than the whole south. These pedestrian-elites are quick to assert the identity of their people to gain sympathetic but often irrational support from their tribesmen while condemning the so-called tribalism of others. In this case, President Muhammadu Buhari is the tribalist to them. Hypocrites! Why don't you check yourselves first?

However, there is no doubt about the fact that certain actions of President Muhammadu Buhari have given strength to the dying arguments of these *biostealthsomatic* tribal merchants. And he has, consciously or consciously, opened himself and other detribalized northern elites to being labelled tribalists and jihadists, because of his chronic and annoying silence in the face of excruciating pains of seeing lunatic herdsmen spill human blood –innocent or guilty.

He cannot imprudently or innocently keep quiet on this issue anymore, if he does, it shall be in his record as a silent supporter of lunatic-killers for generations to come. President Muhammadu Buhari must not just be seen as acting; he MUST take a firm step against these lunatic Fulani-killer-herdsmen.

That said, we must ask ourselves these basic questions: how strong is the state of our union? Do we want to continue to allow these petty, puerile and pedestrian elites to continuously divide us in the name of fighting for tribal security? Can we withstand any genuine external aggression as a people based on our current divided national-psychology of exploitative ethnoreligious sentiments? Or are we trying to deceive ourselves and claim there is nothing like mutual ethnoreligious suspicions? What about 2015 elections: have we, the southerners, forgotten our unfounded fear of Islamization of Nigeria, just because a Fulani General was contesting?

However, when a Southern General a Yoruba Christian contested in 1999 we did not sing such high pitched hypocritical songs of fear; why? If we read our history, we will remember the ease with which the British imperialists conquered many nation-states in pre-colonial-Nigeria, just because of internal disharmony of those nations. Do we remember? Don't this inglorious brood of vipers know that no nation has ever been conquered from outside until it has ruined itself from within?

But how do we fight an enemy who is so formless as to be nothing even in his something?

What we must know is that tribalism mixed with religious sentiments is the virus for Nigeria's degenerative stagnation and the carriers of this *deadly virus are the* pedestrian elites. The enemies blindfolded by malignant greed, and we must fight them with superior values of respect for every man and woman, with emphasis on objective meritocracy and the common good of the people of the federal republic of Nigeria.

We, the people of Nigeria, must know that a name is merely a tag; a title is just a label, and the colour is a necessary but unsolicited accident; character, however, is the true reflection and identifier of the real person beneath these surfaces.

So, we must know these ethnocentric exploiters for who they are; our enemies and nothing more. We must not be deceived by the title they carry and the language they speak or the religion they practise; those are distractions from the real issues. Those are petty things they use to exploit us and then dump us when they win and assume office. We must see beyond the colours with which they re-paint reality.

If we were to be in the 1940s up to late 1950s, the period preceding our independence from the abominable British imperialists, we would still have been the territorial slave of London and the economic dairy-cows of the loathsome English crown.

Chapter 17

THE EXIT

We Nigerians do not have the exclusive claim to high religiosity as though that is not known to other people, in one form or the other, in many parts of this 21st-century world. Neither do we swim, exclusively, in an ocean of unnecessarily negative-ethnicism conceived, created and stoked up by divisive and sadistic-ruling elites.

These phenomena are found all over the world in varying degrees. Indeed, among the ruling elites, they are found in abundance. However, the thoughts of the elites on these illnesses –racism, tribalism, fascism and insane religiosity- are *mostly mirrored* in the consciousness of the diverse populations of different nations, including the so-called 'western world' led by the USA, the UK, Germany and France, though they all claim to be secular, fair and free states.

For example, three of the nations mentioned above, in spite of their international evils –real or imagined, have reduced varied madness and exploitations associated with unrestrained racism (and all sorts of malicious *indentityisms*) and the insanely-flawed religiosity found in nations *that suspend the efficient* employment and deployment of the divine gift of rationality. They did it by, somewhat, progressively maiming and crippling these monsters through continuous structured and noble adoption of *rationality* in evolving strong institutions that work for the good of the majority of their populations.

Note, however, that racism (especially colour-based bias) is not dead and irrational religiosity of various forms are alive among the lower and higher echelons in their societies. In other words, the evils of these biases are only reduced, not exterminated and can still be felt and touched. And many of their leaders still find the 'backdoor' to exploit these sentiments to psyche-up those who are susceptible to them.

So, these biases may be crippled, but their *cancers* still breathe behind the walls of many lives. With the help of deranged but popular leaders they can easily become a menace once again in the societies concerned. A typical example is the ongoing (since November 2016) *'low-intensity political tribal war'* in the US. It's fueling a 'regressive-primitive' identity politics.

Notwithstanding the flavours of their racial biases –real or imagined, no one can convincingly deny the fact that over the years their *structured-*

thinking and bold-action approach in running state affairs and strengthening public institutions without necessarily abandoning every Judeo-Christian value upon which their nations were founded, has led them to where they are today in terms economic, political and structural developments. You don't have to accept my style of expression, but you cannot deny this fact.

God, if you like, transforms their societies using the very power he shares with humanity: the power of reasoning in all its higher forms. Of course, they have their shameful extremes, too. They sentimentally shrink morality for political correctness and maliciously *deified* rationality in order to attack what they misunderstand or don't like about genuine religious values. In other words, they resort to vainglorious intellectual arrogance when dealing with the higher values which religion and nature bestow on human society.

However, irrespective of what you think about them in that aspect, they have elevated and dignified religion more than we do. Why did say that? Because they did not turn religion into a mere emotive nagging science of stagnation. They did not turn religion into an obstructive science that would have senselessly abandoned their fate and the development of their nations to God (by praying and fasting) when they ought to be getting their 'hands dirty', erecting developmental projects, and getting their heads occupied with the calculation about the precise direction forward for the greater good of their peoples.

Elevated and Liberated Religiosity

Thus, the pedestrian religiosity currently brewed by religionomists and encouraged and promoted by polithiefians and sponsored by economic terrorists cannot take us anywhere near the future our founding fathers envisioned for Nigeria and its people.

As a nation with huge potentials, this cross-fertilization of madness going on in our religious orientation across the length and breadth of Nigeria will neither make us develop at the pace we ought to nor make us holier or fully rational as we should. Instead, we risk becoming more repulsive to the true God of Creation.

A properly nurtured religious intelligence would have questioned the aberrations that spin money for all these undying embers from the pit of hell. These are embers that enslave the minds and souls of many by forging shackles from the Holy

Scriptures and reinforcing them with aggressive psychologically deceptive marketing.

If we were to be in the 1940s up to late 1950s, the period preceding our independence from the abominable British imperialists, we would still have been the territorial slave of London and the economic dairy-cows of the loathsome English crown. Why, because these confused religionomists and their allies would have told us, 'God will fight for us, just wait and see'; and we, either because of our collective religious insanity or individual delusion, would have waited for a non-existent warrior-god. None sense!

Our founding fathers, the people who fought for the liberation of Nigeria, never did that they adopted the gifts of God in them and achieved their dream of an independent country. These people, Obafemi Awolowo, Nnamdi Azikiwe, Tafa Balewa and so forth, trusted God but deployed the tactical weapons of *reason* and *pragmatic* steps since God won't do the possible, he does only the impossible.

These men had a religion, yet when they had to fight for the liberation of Nigeria from the greedy British imperialists, they did not sleep in their religious safe house(s) just because an elevated idiot called a man of God said so. They did not turn God into a battering ram against the British imperialists because a fame-hunter-turned-seer claimed God will fight for them. No, God did his part and they, as freedom fighters, actively and rationally pushed for what they believed was right and necessary: the independence of Nigeria, and they got it. Their actions dignified religion and advanced genuine reliance on God more than what we currently see all around.

It is a shame that instead of advancing a dignifying and elevated image of religion we are busy promoting the repulsive idea of religion in the manner that thrusts everything at the feet of religion or its god/God.

Religion is just one of the dimensions of humanity, not the whole of the dimensions. Religion is now confused for magic. Therefore, religion is drawn more and more into the realm of superstition. The tiny and almost imaginary line between religion and superstition disappears every second in Nigeria. Why, because illegitimate and greedy marketers of religion are becoming increasingly aggressive in packaging madness in the garment of religious piety.

I have never seen or read or heard of any scripture so abused for pecuniary gains by those interpreting it like the Bible. Of course, the imams are catching up, too, in the case of Quranic misinterpretation. If Christian clerics can build mansions upon mansions and own fleets of automobiles for talking nonsense in the name interpreting the Holy Bible, they think, 'then we, Nigerian imams, too, can do it, God will understand'. What a crazy company of holy thieves in the cloak of piety!

I challenge you, thieves, in 'the sanctuary' to adjust your way and give religion the image it deserves.

Religion is a genuine medium of encounter and connection with the Father of all creation, and a mechanism for rising beyond the base desires of life without insulting the Divine gifts of *will* and *reason,* gifts implied by Genesis 1:26-27.

Religion doesn't and must not abandon the mandate given to man at creation in Genesis 1:28-30 which suggests that we should consciously do our part in the ongoing (re)creation of our life as a nation with our whole being. Enough of this alliance of madness that is ruining our life as a nation through the exploitation of the religious desires of our people.

Religion cannot take the place of a *structured-thinking and bold-action approach* to development in science, technology and the economy; just as this bold approach can NEVER take the place of religion. A human being is a multi-dimensional being, and his incorporeal and mortal dimensions must not be confused for one another. Neither of the dimensions must be used to exploit the other. Instead, as an alternative, each dimension of man must be sustained for proper integration which leads to a fully evolving yet un-evolved man; the good-man with multi-dimensions all working harmoniously for his good and the good of others.

We must understand that a religion with crippled rationality leads to violent superstition or fanaticism of various forms, and 'high' rationality without the element of (theistic beliefs) religion snowballs into dry atheism or militant hatred of genuine religious values. It follows, therefore, that an authentic religion, if properly practised, will all always lead to rational evolution and development of higher values for human advancement. This is a fact of human history.

Real religion itself is an embodiment and fulfilment of reason and as well as the expression of reason. Documented and oral ancient philosophy of various traditions will remind you how genuine continuous religious speculations helped in advancing the evolution of articulated or methodic thinking.

However, effort should be made by genuine women and men of God and religious people of various traditions, especially Christians and Muslims, to give more articulate analysis of religious beliefs and suffocate religionomists and other exploiters of religion in the public space. We can do this by reducing or, if possible, by removing altogether the attitude of turning God into battering ram in almost every circumstance. It is a ridiculous approach to religion. It does not make God more divine, instead, it insults his divine wisdom more. Why should God be used as a battering ram, even when it is so obvious that what the prevailing situation needs is just for one or two honest clerics and a handful of godly elites to speak out against the abuse of power?

Dear clerics, encourage your congregations to know the broad line between 'the needed' human actions and the divine 'intervention'. It is only by doing this that religion is elevated, not by reinforcing people's servile understanding of God.

For instance, the late Gani Fawehimi (SAN) was not a cleric; he was a fiery constitutional lawyer, human right activist and a faithful Muslim. His actions were against all forms of abuse of power by those in authority, the so-called Nigerian establishment. Even under the murderous Abacha regime, he spoke out against injustice, while many clerics and useless politicians were busily exploiting the situation. He, not those useless clerics elevated religion, especially Islam, far more than 20,000 pedestrian imams and pastors all over Nigeria. Though I am Catholic, he showed me how to blend faith, profession and action for the good of others without being preposterous. So, stop saying or praying that God should remove Buhari, your governor or any public office holder. That is superstitious. It is anti-religious and anti-rational.

God will not remove your governor, senator, Buhari or any other public office holder for that matter. It is our duty; so let's go do it with well-reasoned calculations. To get God involved you will have to do your part.

Since many people don't think outside what many of you clerics tell your congregations, you will have to encourage your people to get their permanent voter's cards, convince one or two persons in their area of influence to support or not to support a particular candidate on pure moral, existential, economic and developmental bases.

They should not vote for someone because he is an *aboki* from the north or because he says, 'Allahu Akbar.' Neither should they vote for someone because he is from the south and says, 'In Jesus

Name' otherwise these people (politicians) will win those offices again with landslides and God will do nothing. He will do nothing by doing something: laughing at your collective childish charades. It is a *special kind of doing* something. It is not because he is incapable of drawing the carpet beneath your enemies' feet but because you are *respectable clowns* leading half-brain legions. God won't be 'more divine' by endorsing our fantasies and act like magicians in situations we need to use our brains and ask for the grace to take the right step and get the work done. No, God is Divine irrespective of our misrepresentation of his 'divineness'.

Moving Forwards Together in Rational Diversity

Having breathed the air and drank the water of five out of the six geopolitical zones[1] in Nigeria and established the brotherhood of common humanity that crosses the ethnic boundaries, I dare say that, there is nothing wrong with rational or positive-ethnic consciousness. What is irredeemably wrong and evil is negative or irrational-ethnicism (or irrational ethnic consciousness).

By irrational or negative-ethnicism, I mean the group consciousness that sees itself as exceptional and, therefore, expects that all other groups with their values, cultures, interests and worldviews must be damned or dominated in every circumstance that brings them even remotely in contact with it.

The negative-ethnicism is irrational since it sees reality from a unidirectional or a parallel dimension only. In other words, they see everything from their point of view alone. They ignore or stifle every-and-any attempt to see reality in the slightest sense from the angles of other group-consciousness.

Rational or positive-ethnicism, on the other hand, refers to the group consciousness that sees itself as unique and distinct but deals with other groups with respect and honour they deserve because it sees reality from the multidirectional spectrum or horizontal-vertical dimension. Consequent upon this mental attitude, it always attempts to see every situation or reality from the angles of other groups even in the slightest of circumstances that bring it in contact with the interests, values, cultures and worldviews other than its own.

It is, therefore, necessary to note that, preserving and protecting all ethnic groups in Nigeria, irrespective of their religious affiliation, is not just important, it is a sacred duty of all -both the government and the governed. These groups, whether you like their cultures or not, as long as they respect and preserve the dignity of the human person in its most sacred form in their value systems, contribute to the cultural and value ecosystem of Nigeria, and thus they must be protected.

If a particular group is tactically suppressed continuously, there will be dangerous degenerative effects or consequences on our national socio-cultural and politico-economic ecosystem. In fact, we are witnessing that already.

Of course, being rational about our ethnicity does not mean we do not have a different view of life as influenced by our cultural milieu. We are different indeed, even though we are all human beings and equal in dignity. Yet, in spite of the differences in our cultural and social orientations, we all have the same fundamental desire that lies deep at the core of our common humanity, that is, the desire to live peacefully in progressive abundance.

This cut across all races, ethnicities or tribes anywhere, everywhere and every time. Only an animal of the lowest order in human skin will joyfully stir up *wars and strifes* within and among the people who would have lived forever peacefully and joyfully without ever forging a sword in spite of their ethnoreligious differences.

If Nigeria is to fulfil its destiny as an active part of history-shaping nations that is the mouthpiece for and the Giant of Africa, we must recognise and accept our differences in the positive sense. This will allow us to emphasize only what unites us and categorize our differences as accidents of our co-existence, not the essence of our destiny to evolve a peaceful, cohesive and progressive Nigeria under God. Hence, if we are to move forward as a force for the greater good, then it is necessary and indispensable for us to move forward with rational/positive ethnic consciousness.

If the rainbow were to have one colour, it wouldn't have had the appeal it has from generations to generations. So, there is just no way we can move forward together if we can't state the fact as fact and an opinion as opinion before asserting the right of any group.

We can't move forward together as a force for good if we, the people, always allow the political elites and all their affiliates to manipulate our collective emotion.

We can't become a cohesive and peaceful nation under God if we allow them to control our intelligence to support their regressive, immoral and evil ethnicism that furthers their abominable and accursed political careers or their ongoing class domination.

Exit Points: The Descent or The Ascent?

On Saturday the 21st of February 2015, I was invited to Splash FM, Ibadan, by Edmund Obilo, a well-rounded and fiery investigative journalist, to feature on his famous live radio programme, 'Voices' *-the state of the nation.*

After a couple of questions relating to my harsh critique of the defective ethnoreligious orientation of many Nigerians, he finally quoted a line from *Irresponsible God or Foolish Worshippers or A Confused Nation,* which was a title of one of my letters (or articles) to him, and then he looked at me and asked, "why did you use such harsh words?"

Well, my response to him was simple. I just repeated the same quotation he read to me verbatim, "...because in Nigeria every *idiot is a pastor even a dog is, every fool is an imam even a goat is and every mentally deranged person is a prophet....*" That was then.

And now, three years later, I ask myself over and over again, "have I been proven right or wrong?" Surely, that's left for anyone who understands the current 'ethnoreligious terrains' of Nigeria to answer.

I think we can delude ourselves and claim '*God's Will*' will prevail in this country while we 'hunt and drag' each other down the path of destruction. I don't have a problem with that claim anyone can claim anything. But I will ask you, what do we mean by 'God's *will* will prevail' for a people who have foolishly or ignorantly canonized the ascent of religionomists and polithiefians, and (sub)consciously legitimized the descent of a rationally responsible God in public their lives?

Surely, it means nothing more than accelerated poverty and a delusional bright future. We keep destroying inter-ethnic trust and reinforcing insane ethnoreligious distrust by building communication obstructing walls of sentiments. And, then, we say God will help us because 'his *will*' will prevail. That's amusing, to put it mildly.

We do all we can as a people to consciously disturb 'God's siesta' with our irritating nocturnal noises. Our irrelevant arguments and excuses as to why a morally and rationally responsible God should do what he has empowered us to do right from the moment of our creation without doing our part. Why should he do it? If he does what we are capable of doing, then he must either be mad or be irresponsible. Or he is not the God at all, but a mere sick god.

We have allowed our 'subconscious-self' to be conditioned to seeking help from God for socio-political and ethnoreligious issues that even our ancestors in their majestic primitiveness would have solved through dialogue, natural justice and the emphasis on the principle of corrective justice.

We now enthrone an insane god with his ministers –religionomists and polithiefians- by seeking from without that which is in abundance within us, and by so doing we enrich the fake ministers *and weaken our capacity to put up stiff resistance against* the continuous abuse of power and looting of our collective treasure and draining of our commonwealth by perforating the national treasury.

We become impoverished as a nation in spite of the humungous and unparalleled wealth the Creator has endowed us with. And as individuals, our lives become more of a burden than a joyous experience. Isn't the joy of life in living life abundantly in progressive peace? How do you live life abundantly, when the wealth of the land is cornered and, for the most part, ferried away to countries which only remember our leaders are corrupt when they want to keep us in line?

Yet those countries which our own certified and professional bastards called leaders, both clerics and politicians, ferry our commonwealth to, insult us arrogantly, by saying we, Nigerians, are fantastically corrupt. What arrant nonsense!

Who is more corrupt between a bank thief and the police officer who helps him escape and keep the stolen money in his police barracks' apartment? The billions of pounds and dollars stolen from the people of Nigeria and kept in the banks of the West -from London to New York and from Switzerland to

France- are locked away in 'the vaults of their economies' providing jobs to their citizens. These billions are, to a verifiable extent, contributing their economies, making life more meaningful for a huge number of their citizens and, of course, their nations are richer for it.

Then our brothers and sisters, uncles and aunts, fathers and mothers, in spite of their academic or technical qualifications, literally beg to enter those countries to earn a living while still contributing to the growth of those economies and, at the same time, depriving Nigeria of these priceless human assets.

'Imperialists' are perpetually tyrants. It doesn't matter whether the version of the tyranny of imperialism is homegrown or foreign; religious or political; military or physical; politico-financial neocolonialism or direct colonialism. The important point is, 'imperialism' rules and exploits you to the breaking point. Unfortunately, our current homegrown imperialists seem to have our 'PIN codes', and they will milk us till death until we say *enough is enough* and act accordingly.

It is sad to see the religion that should be challenging its adherents to think outside the box as they pray now emphasizing a boxed-thinking. And it's also elevating *prayer-solves-it-all* and *God-will-intervene* in ideology. This is an ongoing disaster and an insult to our collective intelligence.

When the so-called *men of god* (?) ought to speak out boldly against oppressive policy, they check first to see if the arrowhead of the policy belongs to their *religious dessert* or ethnic menu before attempting to clear their throats and then say, "let's pray for our leaders, it is not easy".

Excuse me. Of course, it is easy. If not, they should just get out of the place and let other people in. Simple. What an incredulous hordes are these religionomists? They hardly think beyond their pockets. Scandalous and irritating!

Well, they may say their prayers to the marines! Hypocrites! It is not easy, yet they are ready to die in office if allowed.

Ethnoreligious consideration is often employed in looking at circumstances that should be viewed through issue-based lenses only. One would expect that these self-serving and self-proclaimed men of god, both beneath the Cross and behind the Crescent, should at least challenge the arrogance of those in power by simply saying the truth promptly and constantly and nothing more. But instead of doing that they start seeing (from their convention grounds or camp meetings) *some delusional visions of abundance where we have sown nothing as a people.*

Therefore, if the old lies of these so-called ministers of 'God' (religionomists) are now the new truths, and the truths of the reality staring us in the eyes every minute are lies; then, it is either because they have not reflected enough on Amos 5:21-27; 8:4-4 and Philippians 3:19 and then re-contextualize these passages, by inserting themselves, their offspring and cohorts in the whole drama' as they *become* the new 'targets of Divine rebuke. Or it may be because they have become sophisticated *rogues in the sanctuary* and care little about the impacts of their abuse of religion. In other words, these religious leaders have simply grown old in their wickedness, and they either have never had contact with or have lost touch with God who is always ready to be on the side of the manipulated, the exploited and the oppressed[1].

Consequently, I can say by *their fruit we know them*[2], their habitually hypocritical but devastating silence in the face of the abuse of power by politicians with deep pockets who mess with the lives of the citizens of this country through their inhuman or anti-people, pro-elites policies suggests there is a (descent or) fall of a morally and rationally responsible God from their lives. They have nothing in common with God; they are far from Christ Jesus. They raised their egos to the heavens; it is about them, their families and cohorts, ultimately, not about God.

Their version of 'Jesus' died and they rose in his place, and so they seek to possess, dominate and control people by whatever means but in the most benign way possible. That is why their *gospel* has only Matthew 26:3-4 in which they perpetually repeat their conspiracy *against Jesus in the people* (Mathew 25:40), because they 'ally' themselves with the politicians and all who oppress the people, including their flocks.

Therefore, as it stands, the (domination and) ascent of the *religionomists* and *moneyticians* is now a fact of history, not a mere circumstantial experience. But where we go from here and how we get there is up to us all.

Remember, ultimately, all I have done in this book, in my reflections, is to prompt everyone to stop boxed-thinking religiosity, regressive ethnicism and subservient approach to our political our participation. It will not help us if we continue on that path. It will ruin us, for sure.

Religion cannot and must not be suppressed for the sake of political correctness; it will make us soul-less animals with nothing transcendence to order the society towards. And that is dangerous, it always is.

The ethnicity of people is part of their socio-psychological make-up, a powerful safety net of some sort and an expression of who they are. So it must not be denied or taken away from them, just because we want everyone to look like us, it will always lead to violence and resistance. If God wanted us all to look alike, then he would have instructed the 'nature' to condition us that way.

Yet, boxed religionism and ethnic jingoism must not be allowed to dominate our politics, interactions and social relationships; they reign on people's raw emotions with less, if any, space for rational control once they take root in their lives. And wherever people have been continually primed by various means to be susceptible to the influence of these regressive phenomena, the 'elites' and politicians are known to exploit such circumstance with ease.

Finally, we need to understand that boxed-religious consciousness and negative ethnicism are very contagious and very explosive. Therefore, we must rise above them and assert our right to question those in authority irrespective of the religion they profess or their ethnic affiliation. Without that, the 'right crooked' person(s) will always rule us.

But we need leaders, not rulers, and they must be the right persons.

ACKNOWLEDGEMENTS

Special thanks to every non-partisan, blunt and analytic journalist who has made every effort to encourage the people to think more outside the box and ask more questions about how our life, as a people, is being managed by our leaders –both religious and secular- and challenge their often deceptive *official narratives*.

Edmund Obilo readily comes to mind here, and I say, 'Keep up the good works'. Thanks, too, to Fr. Basikoro Cyril Dase for your comments about the earlier draft of this book they led to considerable improvements.

Finally, I say special 'Thank You' to Mr Odidere Maria Adeojo for your *one in a million* support. I appreciate you always.

APPENDIX

[Reflections from the Past]

FELA WAS A PROPHET, TOO.

Mr. Edmund, on the last edition of Voices (28:02:2015), you brought a man who claimed to be an apostle or prophet. Well, anyone can claim to be anything and, according to the intellectual tradition I belong, we or rather I believe that you call people what they call themselves without necessarily believing in what they call themselves. Mr Edmund read my lips, if you can through these texts; your *prophet is a dreamer.*

You are a prophet in your own right, a journalistic prophet. And you are an apostle in your own right, an apostle of *truth, justice and tactical mind mending.* We have classes of prophets; let us leave that for another day. But I know that Fela (Baba Abami Eda) was a prophet, and Gani Fawehinmi was a *prophet.*

Note, Mr Radio man, these men like the real prophets sought no tacit or pronounced fame, what they stood for transcended money, fame and power which are the most subtle but efficient reasons religion involuntarily employs more shafts among grains and more wolves in lamb's skin.

His so-called *predictions* are nothing but predictions.

Prophecy, technically speaking, is not a prediction. Any idiot can predict a situation based on some strands of undercurrent events, clear events and anticipated events. Thus, for someone claiming he read the Revelation in order to interpret Obama's emergence, was funny.

In fact, I was cocksure of his emergence back then, all you needed to do was to study and follow the crazy American socio-political orientation and the voting pattern of that beautifully *rotten apple* called America.

Your apostle cum prophet probably was seeing events through coca cola bottle and he, probably, supposed the (whole) listeners of your programme or the whole world reason with their religious emotions or think through some olive oil miracle.

If not, he would not have engaged in some puerile premises that weaken his predictions in my ear or the ears of even people of socio-political average intelligence.

See Mr Edmund, your guest-apostle claimed he predicted the emergence of Jacob Zuma. Tell me, who was strong enough to assume that office when Thabo Mbeki was forced to resign?

Who was strong enough to break the so-called legacy party of Mandiba – the ANC- as at 2009/2010, and even as at the last year 2014 elections- in South Arica? Julius Malema or that woman whose name I cannot remember right now? Or Zuma's deputy who was not in control of the regional and Trade Union' party structures?

It was obvious to us or me that no one else as at that time in history can become South African President. So, what was the world transforming predictions he made that he was referring to?

Was his god not some all knowing-god? Why did he not predict Ahmid Kasai of Afganistan tenure's end and the near-disaster that the disagreement between the two most prominent candidates of that *little hell republic* in Asia (almost led to)?

These people should occupy themselves with more productive thinking and rationally inspiring speculation, not some empty, jaundice-infected and delusion-engulfed predictions. Even the *Boko Harramites* can predict the total disintegration of Nigeria because that will make the news headlines, thereby giving them some *polythene-fame*. And, maybe, some thread of control over a bunch of *firewoods for stoking the flame of servitude*.

Nobody from the East of the Niger will become president this year or next year; except, of course if by next year his sick god/God means 2019.

Your Ardent Listener,

Me

2nd March 2015

RETHINKING GOD IN GOVERNANCE

If the federal and state governments in Nigeria are not having a minus one (-1) in their mathematics of governance, they should by now know that the problem with the nation is not that God is so mean and vengeful to the point that he preoccupies himself with our sins. Rather, if there was anything relating to sins at all in our suffering, as we are covertly being made to believe by various senseless support and sponsorship of religious programmes by government functionaries (I guess it is meant to either appease the dead gods or play on people's emotions), it is the sin of refusal of the political leaders and their cohorts *in and outside of* the corridors of power to employ their brains (if those are working well anyway) and find necessary solutions to Nigeria's clustering problems.

Solving Nigeria's problems does not need rocket scientists. All it needs is just Structured Thinking Bold Action -STBA. Bold action that is less psycharcinogenic and more genuinely pro-masses and patriotic. Enough of this senseless struggle for political and public offices with which you bunch of miserable lot have done more evil to Nigeria and Nigerians than good.

Your rational faculties should be finding ways of reducing wastages caused by your bogus salaries and allowances that are nothing but Sodomitan fire and brimstones on your abominable Gomorran purses and accounts.

The political elites push prayers and malicious ethnicity to the populace while they battle for the money-spinning positions from Edo to Ondo, from Ekiti to Ebonyi, Kogi to Kwara, Zamfara to Sokoto, Kaduna to Kano, Nassarawa to Adamawa, Borno to Benue, from Cross River to Rivers and; from Anambra to Abuja. It is as though God is now a magical household idol that will help the people while they (il)legally rob the nation of its wealth.

Of course, having prayer sessions for the nation when things aren't going the right way is not too bad, but it is irredeemably bad when these sessions are encouraged tacitly or expressly by those enemies of our collective progress who hide under the garments of politics but whose hearts are filled with dishonesty, their brains coloured with ignorance, ineptitude, indifference and intolerance.

That's why at the federal level the likes of Saraki and Dogara will stop at nothing to 'stay in their seats', despite the fact that their presence in those seats is nothing but *a political sacrilege against those 'sacred' seats.* Those seats, I agree, are not reserved for saints, because the last saintly politician died a long time ago, but the seats are for people who are humble enough to acknowledge the fact that the vast majority of Nigerians need quality and self-evaluating leaders who are never indifferent to agonizing pains of Nigerians.

The leadership of the National Assembly, of course, reflects the general composition of both houses as nothing but, to a nauseating great degree, a boardroom of opportunity entrepreneurs and legislative asylum seekers and social security scavengers.

Otherwise, what are the likes of David Mark, Godswill Akpabio, and other ex-governors with ruinously bogus pensions doing there? Dino Melaye and the gangs are not left out too, to mention just a few. Why can't they stay back in their mosques, churches and cult-houses and talk to their deities for insights, if they have decided to have lesser brain cells? The National Assembly without empathy for the populace is not better than a disease-infested cocoa pod.

In any case, the list of Nigeria's problems is endless though lawlessness is at the centre of that, virtually everyone, including the man on the street and our dear power grabbers, knows the most pressing ones.

For example, the menace of corruption across the nation; maybe Boko Haram in the Northeast; youth restiveness in the Niger Delta region and other youth dominated crises and their attendants destruction of lives and properties, just to list a few, clearly show the whole reasoning world that successive governments in Nigeria have done terrible things by doing nothing for the systematic development of Nigerian youths and Nigeria as a whole.

Another example of the most basic thing everyone knows it needs urgent and unmediated attention is the erratic power supply. If there was anything that I hated most while in Nigeria, it was the epileptic power supply. And it is so cancerous and destructive to industrial cum economic development of the people and the nation that everyone is getting more involved in the commercial aspect of the economy than in production/manufacturing aspect which is the real sector of any modern economy. No serious countries ever attain their potentials in this manner, selling for the manufacturing countries!

Anyone can be a president, but not all presidents can rationally rethink governance in a gradual but progressive manner for the Good of the Masses. Obasanjo administration (May 29,1999- May 29, 2003) thought that by changing the name of the organization responsible for the (national grid) generation, transmission and distribution of electricity in the country will reduce the problems of epileptic power supply and maybe eventually eradicate power epilepsy soon.

Consequently, he changed their name from NEPA, which for the ordinary but great people of Nigeria meant *Never Expect Power Always*, to PHCN Plc (i.e. Power Holding Company of Nigeria). And alas, true to the new name they actually held power. Of course, the hidden truth was that the bastards were planning to sell our patrimony, our commonwealth to a bunch of successful idiots in the name of efficient administration.

Well, based on the reality of the *Abiku nature* of power supply, this new name (PHCN Plc) meant *only and only* one thing to every Nigerian on the street, whether they can or can't afford an I-Pass-my-Neighbour generator, *a continuation of woes.*

So for the people, PHCH plc meant *power has changed name please light candles*, what a creative people Nigerians can be with their sorrows, even at their lowest point. Hmm, 9ja for real.

It was not a surprise to me that NEPA's name was changed. No, because history well understood brightens the mind and widens your thoughts compass making it a logical multidimensional thinking incorporeal organism. I was not surprised at all, I just hated the whole system of deception with passion.

The change of the name of an important agency of the government of a country that can afford to budget billions yearly for the *damned generators of its president(s)* and others beneficiaries, with neither strategic thinking nor evidently emerging efficiency, shows the very template of a political class that think less of the process of governance but talk more of politics. And also it reveals how these political entrepreneurs think in reality that changing parties' names and logos are the major ways of getting politically efficient; a sad sign of a privileged class with unprivileged rational capacity that makes them oscillate between political superstition and meaningful political rationality.

When Jonathanian administration came on board PHCN Plc went dancing, by that l mean PHCN was partitioned among political Scavengers and Co., arbitrarily employing appropriate legal mechanisms, oh boy smart kids! So PHCN became DISCO! Wow!

If only Nigerian leadership or the federal government knows that God is on vacation as far as Nigeria political prayer sessions are concerned, l just hope they do, those in *Aso-Rock* will not bother wasting our money to do any covert sponsorship of any senseless prayer sessions for things God has given them enough thinking cap to do.

If the political class, especially in the corridors of power, knows that Nigeria's problem does not worth disturbing God's 'vacation' for, as far as Nigeria's political infertility and jerky-progress are concerned because God in his infinite love for us as a nation has given us all we need to develop every aspect of our life as a country, they probably will devise a more dignifying way of continuing their overt and covert religious charades instead of the senseless show of shame we see among the political class all the time.

Since the celebration of the so-called democracy day of 1999 till today our life as a nation, or country depending on your view, has been that of a jerky-progress, if I can call it progress anyway. However, the government at all levels in Nigeria should know and note that they need to seriously rethink what it means for a country to progress economically and if they don't know what to think they should just start empowering the people, not through okada but stable electricity and the result will be amazing.

Among Nigeria's problems power stability remains the only one that can solve 1,001 problems within four years. But what were the scavengers that ruled instead of leading Nigeria from May 29 1999 - May 29, 2014, able to achieve in the first 15 years of return to 'Osicracy' or 'paupercracy' or democracy as most of you will call it?

Years ago, I used to wonder, back then when (in Nigeria) various governments of those periods were more of extensions of certain religions if they knew that the people of tiny Republic of Togo, too, pray but work harder to generate 9,000 megawatts as at 2011. Ghana within that period too had a population of around 24,000,000 and generated about 8,000 megawatts; South Africa had a population of about 54,000,000 and generated about 46,000 megawatts between those periods of our 1999-2014.

Still in that same period of excess crude dollars, blind lootings and petty political-religionism and lazy thinking politicians in Nigeria, Brasil had a population of about 180,000,000, the most populous of the Latins, generated about 90,000 megawatts but Nigeria with the political elites who were and are giants of poverty and generators of irresponsibility, graciously generated 4,300 megawatts for close to 155,000,000 people.

Around of applause for them. Let's Clap for our politicians, that was a great feat, indeed. It means about 9,000,000 people will share 300 megawatts! While with simple calculation in South Africa around that same period only about 1,200,000 people will share 1,000 megawatts!

Now, in 2017 two years into the government of change has anything changed? Has it? You may answer the question. Of course, I know it is a known fact that it is always easy to destroy but difficult to rebuild. Yet, what efforts are being put in place to give us infrastructural hope, especially in the area of a stable power supply? I don't want to talk about injustice this is not one-reflection-cover-it-all.

You know, sometimes, l can't but wonder why those at the helms of affairs in Nigeria (Aso Rock and State Government Houses) cannot bother to think logically or at least pay people to think coherently for the Common Good.

In the final analysis, if most of these psycharcinogenic political elites can go inwards on a logical thinking trip and, put the results of that thorough trip to work then they can pray to God for blessing.

However, if they keep looking for a short-cut by suspending their rational faculty, a gift of God, meant for governing properly in manners that make the proverbial milk and honey flow ceaselessly, then, they can go to hell with their ever-present tendency to appeal to religious sentiments of the people and perhaps their Gods.

If our politicians will always run away from *reasoning a path forward for the country,* then they have no right to disturb God since has endowed us with great potentials from different angles.

Originally written for and published on: 'Democracy Day', May 29, 2017.
Available at: http://femiscythingpen.blogspot.com/2017/05/

FEEDBACK APPRECIATED

For comments, analysis and recommendations, you can reach the author via femifeedback@yahoo.com

Thank you!

OTHER BOOKS BY THE AUTHOR

Now available online / Amazon.com

- **THE RED ONION PSYCHOLOGY: Inflections or Reflections (Volume One)**
-

End Notes

Chapter 1

Religion Gone Rogue

[1] These were mere theoretical official theories or policies of states such as The Soviet Union, North Korea, Communist China and Cuba but the majority of people on the ground have their religious convictions different from their governments.

[2] Though some nations are referred to as developed, I think that's merely an arrogant intellectual expression. They may be advanced in many ways but not developed. Perhaps they should say what that means, because they want us to associate with something unidirectional.

If they were developed, why were they building new roads; new schools; new bridges; battling housing problems for the homeless and fighting the regression in basic moral sanity? Why upgrade the infrastructures generally and so on? Every living nation is either developing or regressing; evolving or facing extinction; Living or dying.

[3] National Bureau of Statistic, (no date) *Population 2006-2016*. Available at: https://nigerianstat.gov.ng/elibrary?queries[search]=population (Accessed: 25, July 2019).

[4] *Crude oil…like the abused oil endowed states of Niger Delta…*

This statement is merely a metaphor that points to reality; the wasting of human potentials of most Nigerians. However, Delta State is actually located in the south-south geo-political zone of Nigeria, in spite of its huge oil reserves it is one of the most environmentally devastated states in Nigeria because of impact oil spillages etc.

[5] See the Gospel of St. John 8:32 *You shall know the Truth and the Shall set you free.*

[6] Of course, the followers themselves are dangerously confused about what the roles of leaders are in the society and their own responsibilities as followers to act when the need arises. Unfortunately, a chunk of Nigerian media (sometimes behaves like the often arrogant and elitist western media –of UK, US, Germany, Australia, French etc) that is supposed to be mending and sharpening objective minds of the people is, subtly partisan or completely bought. Just some section of Nigerian media, not all the media, unlike in the West where their so-called independent media are more less the back doors for government mechanisms for controlling the narratives and manipulating the trust of the public in what Noam Chomsky famously termed *manufacturing consent.*

[7] It is a metaphor for some real 'college of evils' in Nigeria there is no bottling company bearing such name here in Nigeria.

Chapter 2

God Of The Universe Is An Intelligent And Responsible Being

[1] It does not mean that all scientists believe in a being called God. But they agree, nonetheless, that the universe is a unique super system which is naturally and efficiently organized.

[2] Simply put, all (matter, energy, place or location in space) things in existence whether on earth or in outer space, whether seen, heard or

known to human beings or not, that is the totality of all matter and energy that exists in the vastness of the created space.

[3] The term 'world' here does not suggest different planets. Instead, it means one planet with different environments and different levels of existence.

[4] It is the study of the universe and the celestial bodies, gas, and dust within it. Astronomy includes observations and theories about the solar system, the stars, the galaxies, and the general structure of space.

[5] The intelligent creator being or mere cosmic force as some would prefer to call it.

[6] I am not concerned with the myopic approach to understanding the natural law as limited to religion, morality and ethics by many. Rather, I am concerned with the inherent law guiding everything created irrespective of size, location or weight.

[7] Of course, theology in Christian contexts deals with or reflects on the Divine Revelation within context of faith community.

[8] There are some levels of arguments among some thinkers, especially metaphysics inclined thinkers, about the use of the words *eternal and everlasting* interchangeably. They argue that eternal means without beginning or end; while everlasting means having beginning but has no end.

[9] The 'he' I constantly use is not to specifically reinforce the general conception of God/Creator-being as a man, rather 'he' is consistently used to avoid the clumsy use of he, she or it as pronouns for the *being* I

am describing. It does not mean a gender specific pronoun but a pronoun of convenience.

[10] See Genesis 1:28

Chapter 3

A Nation In The Wilderness Of Religious Servitude

[1]Embassy of Nigeria, Sweden. “Natural Resources”, *Nigeriaembassy.nu*, 2016. http://nigerianembassy.nu/natural-resources/.

[2] Fawenhimi, Feyi, “A (not so) brief history of the fall and fall of the Nigerian naira”, *Quartz Africa*, 6th December, https://qz.com/africa/564513/a-not-so-brief-history-of-the-fall-and-fall-of-the-nigerian-naira/

[3] See Genesis 1:28

[4] Don’t think of the Europeans here think of men and women on the African continents in positions of power.

[5] A Yoruba appellation for Muslim congregational gathering that usually meets on Sundays under different ‘alfas’ or ‘imams’ or ‘sheiks’.

[6] “Patrick Oliver Sawyer…. flew into Nigeria with the Ebola virus, he was a Liberian-American lawyer who was notable for being the index case for the introduction of Ebola virus disease into Nigeria during the West African Ebola epidemic,” March 6, 2017, https://en.wikipedia.org/wiki/Patrick_Sawyer

[7] Marked by delusions, hallucinations, incoherence, and distorted perceptions of reality.

Chapter 4

Questioning The Basis Of Nigerians' Religiosity

[1] These are founders, owners and managers of various religious houses which are either Islamic or Christian or other religious traditions. They have different titles, and their titles are influenced by what they desire to control, or what they once lacked and which their 'new job' could bring to them.

[2] That is what they say anyway, they are spiritual. But I don't believe them.

[3] The title of the executive is the prerogative of the self-invited, self-called and self-acclaimed men of god or goodies (MoG).

[4] See Philippians 3:19

[5] Anointing here should never be falsely understood in the context of Christianity alone but in the (proper) wider context of 'beliefs' in/of all religion that some men are specially chosen by their deity.

[6] Anthropological tools are preferred here to sociological tools, because it takes a more historical and deep comparative approach than the latter.

[7] It is a Yoruba word coined from a biting Yoruba phrase *se kaa ri mi.* The literal meaning of the phrase is *vainglorious action. Se = to do something; Kaa = so that they (a collection of people); Rii mi = can see me or my action.* It simply means plain show-off or being vainglorious!

[8] There are different categories of poor people in Nigeria, like many nations, too.

[9] If you have never heard of the phrase "performance-enhancing drug", it is a fraudulent drug that is common in the world of sports, especially athletics. It gives the user an unhealthy edge over all other contestants who faithfully or fearfully rely on raw or natural abilities and hard work. The other name for the drug is the *cheat drug.*

[10] There is no genuine, well-thought-out foundational explication and understanding of their core beliefs, and how it is to be followed through. Instead, what you see is an ocean wave of scriptural perception that lacks depth and often inconsistent with scriptural reality itself.

[11] The Nigeria movie industry, the largest in Africa, is collectively called Nollywood. And it seems some aspects of their theology and philosophy of reality are still roaming the woods of ancient syncretism.

[12] It is gibberish. I am just mimicking a lump of names in Arabic, no meaning particular. Just as their business is a religious scam.

[13] These are just formulated or fictitious examples. I doubt if there are religious 'products and services' with these names, at least not that I am aware off. If there is any of such out there then, it is a case of mere coincidence.

[14] By 'republics and kingdoms' I mean their religious houses/centres and subtle or discreet political and business empires they created or are creating out of them.

Chapter 5

Leadership By Accidental Design

[1] A large number of persons occupying positions of authority have proved that we have more of 'leaders' by chance than by choice.

[2] These are either ordinary Nigerians that could not afford travelling abroad or Nigerians who do not believe there can ever be any justifiable reason for them to leave Nigeria or both groups.

[3] Moneyticians, economic-terrorists and religionomists

[4] The deceptive and poisonous mental attitude that has at its heart the aim of spread falsehood that covers malignant desires of a carrier-politicians or individual in public eyes.

[5]Fulani-Invest, here this concept is not talking about money but values inculcated and time or duration of the training and effort made by everyone involved in it, especially the trainee. It's a communal effort, so to speak.

[6] A psycho-theological understanding of Psalm 8, especially 8 verse 5, with Genesis 1:26 reinforces this reality. Man has been empowered to take a lot of decisions in the name of his creator.

[7] This phenomenon is not an exclusively Nigerian issue. My focus, however, is Nigeria's experience interpreted with the mindset of the right place we should have been, had we had visionary and less exploitative leaders.

[8] The concept "followership by accidental-design" means a prevailing situation 'designed' to make the populace believe more in the street *political theology* that tells them that only what God decides is final. Even in the case of public office, their choice does not matter,

they should accept the result of god's decision always, and they believe this with irritating subservience.

Chapter 6

Followership By Accidental-Design

[1] I have no apology to anyone who falls into this class, no excuse, no remorse for the words I used.

[2]Alternating between God and 'god' everywhere in this book is intentional. I want to show that whenever we leave our fates in the hands of irresponsible leaders at all levels because we refuse to do our part, it is not God's fault but our fault or fault of a non-existent *god of inaction.*

[3] No reasonable person will be interested in getting his nation burnt down by taking arms against the state. However, removing any vagabond in power for the good of the greatest majority, especially the suffering youths, needs to be accomplished by whatever peaceful means necessary.

I do not pray for any violence in Nigeria, we have enough of it and it serves no good. I live for what I believe, but I am not afraid of death, death must come one day anyway. So, why not die, if need be, for a greater cause, the reign of progressive abundance?

[4] For example, was it by brutal coincidence that in August 2014 Oritsejafor's jet was used to whisk $9.3m arms deal "raw cash" to South Africa? I don't care about the senseless excuses that were put forward later. I refuse to be fooled.

[5] By 'design' I mean it is planned or preconfigured to work or happen the way it is. It could be as a result of conscious effort or just a circumstantial occurrence.

[6] See Psalm 8:5-8

Chapter 7

Stagnant Nigeria: Who Is To Blame? God, Inept Leaders or Senselessly-Religious And Politically Passive Followers?

[1]Here, in the context of the sovereignty of a state, by 'illegitimate internal manipulation', I mean those who while occupying public offices, twist reality and manufacture 'truths'. They also pit people against each other -divide and rule- and 'sell' their country to *foreign powers* in order to either stay longer in power or get more 'powers' or to steal more and loot the treasury of the state while being patted on the back by their foreign masters who support them from remote lands.

[2] In some sense, it is difficult in this modern world to maintain 100% sovereignty because of factors which include bilateral treaties, extraterritoriality (of embassies), economic dependence etc. These are, however, no excuse for a government to throw its sovereignty to the winds. Or bow to the dictates of other nations at the expense of its national interests.

[3] Our collective wealth is being destroyed by economic-militants in the Niger-Delta region and economic-terrorists in different sections of Nigeria societies, especially those acquiring our commonwealth for themselves by using stolen state resources.

[4] That is the mental power to analyze reality on its own merit and determine its proper place within schemes of (real or possible) things,

even though they are (could be) spiritual, psychological, socio-emotional, intellectual etc.

[5] There is nothing sophisticated about it, but it's perfectly above animal-level intelligence. Human rational power possessed by anyone that is not mentally retarded. It is simple or natural, therefore, not bad yet not very good either.

[6] We share in the divinity of God too, but this is in spiritual planes.

[7] Both the Quran and the Holy Bible asserts that God or Allah created man by breathing into him and told him to give names to other creatures God had created. This is an important transfer of degree of authority to man. See Genesis 2:18-21 &1:26-28

[8] See Psalm 8:3-8

[9] It's a play on two words: Christianity and Islam.

[10]For instance, in the book of Exodus, the Israelites were subjected to terrible servitude. And in Exodus 5:6-14 when they protested and complained to Pharaoh for 'quadrupling' their burdens, there were no positive changes. In that case, any attempt to revolt without a sizeable organized armed or politically viable '*axis of resistance'* would not be beneficial to them. Had they revolted without definite *organized units* with possible chance achieving effective resistance, it would have been a *feast of massacre* for them. *Their wills and intelligence were subdued,* but not taken away, hence, they acted in the most minimal, almost negligible, way and God did the rest through Moses.

So, there was need for *'help' to come from without* to complement their ***desire to be free*** which came *from within.* Yet [emphasis] *they still needed to muster their wills* to (cooperate or) listen and follow the instructions of that 'help' when it was time. Why? Because their wills were only *subdued*, not taken away, therefore, God does only the impossible, not the possible.

[11] Here being *indolent people* does mean that (our) people are lazy as it relates to working to earn their living, no. We, Nigerians, are known everywhere in the world to be hard working souls. What I mean here instead is that people are apathetic, indifferent and bored when it comes to reacting or responding to political issues that directly threaten their daily living and happiness; this is a fact, too.

[12] The west, as currently seen and constituted, is include countries located outside the geographical 'west', although, racially speaking, the so-called 'white' may be the majority of the people. Examples are Canada, Australia and New Zealand etc.

[13] *'Agboode gba foo le Nijiria'* (Yoruba for) the godfathers of the favoured thieves (from Nigeria).

[14] As opposed to *intellectual or rational ethnicity* which sees the uniqueness of a group in the context of its contribution to and appreciation of other groups and their mutual understanding of supportive co-existence.

[15] For lack of better words, they are multifaceted corrupt practices such as nepotism, kickbacks, bribery, office-buying, looting, favouritism, ethnicization of government parastatals etc. These are seen as normal things among many of the elites with warped morality who occupy various offices (secular or religious, public or private). Irrespective of

the nature of the offices in question, to them, whatever they do to remain a privileged class' game, that must be played.

[16] Olalekan, Adetayo. "Meningitis, God's punishment for fornication, Zanfara governor says," *Punch,* April 4, 2017 http://punchng.com/meningitis-gods-punishment-for-fornication-zamfara-governor-says/

[17]Kelechi, Onyemaobi. "Opinion: Meningitis is Not a Divine Punishment," *Eazyfeeds,* 12TH of April, 2017, https://www.eazyfeeds.com.ng/2017/04/opinion-meningitis-is-not-pivine.html.

[18] Psycharcinogenic (*pronounced:* Si-kasii-nojenik) simply means evil-minded or a heartless and callous person. Psycharcinogenic is coined from psyche (mind/soul) +carcinogenic (something with capacity to become or cause cancer/ destructive/poisonous etc).

[19] Sellaoutization (pronounced as *Sell-hoW-Ti-Za shiOn*): Giving out of state owned companies or infrastructure to cronies of those in power in order to enrich themselves at the expense of the state under the guise of privatizing them.

[20] General Buhari is one of those.

[21] Fela Anikulapo-kuti *Beasts of No Nation* was released in 1989.

[22] It has testicles and they dangle nicely. It's a Metaphor, it means something or someone is in the best of shapes.

[23] Fela Anikulapo-kuti's album '*Sorrows, Tears and Blood*' was released in 1977.

[24] Built by the insanely imperial British *foolish-wise men corporation* in 1914 and generously bought by the colonized people of the territory. Now it's our burden and our blessing, depending on how you see it.

Chapter 8

God of Political Prayer Is Dead!

[1]This refers to the societal belief system on (or a general outlook of a people on) any given issues of life.

[2] See Philippians 3:19

[3] Instead of using the *elemental demons* that our politicians use, the Western politicians (especially those of Anglo-Saxon heritage e.g. USA, UK etc) are very good at this act or ***tactics by demonizing other*** nations and people that either better than them or they just don't like e.g. the Russians, Chinese etc. Well, I guess their (Nigerian and Western politicians) aims are the same (blame other people for the very evil you are doing so that your people think less about you and more about your 'enemy') only the objects of their manipulations are different, which I understand.

[4] Psychotic Power-Glue Syndrome or PPGS: Is a deep-seated sickness, as I would say, that many people have, that makes them seek power or access to it or want have relation to those in power or it as a mental obsession with power that makes them want to stay permanently in office, even when without the office, technically speaking, they are politically safe or influential already.

Chapter 9

The Alliance Between Religionomics And The Nigerian Politics

[1] They trade in religion and its many allied phenomena or experiences.

[2] Questioning the veracity of their interest or spiritual faithfulness.

[3] The distortion to this sentence is intentional. It is a verbal jab aimed at emphasizing my firm *objection* to abuse of religious experience. Correct line is: 'start seeing visions and hearing voices'.

[4] Examples abound but they are epitomized by the *bromance* between some clerics likes Ayo-Oritsejafor and former President Jonathan of Nigeria from 2010-15; private jet 'donation' to clerics by people like that etc.

[5]Religionomics (principle of aggressive but shrewd religion marketing): is a purely business principle, approach or orientation espoused by individuals running religious entity or community - churches and mosques etc.

[6]Backwardness here is not in a material sense alone, but more importantly, also it refers to psycho-spiritual and socio-political.

Chapter 10

Politics Is Too Dirty For Upright Men

[1] Allen, J. (no date) *As A Man Thinketh.* Available at: www. librivox.com

[2] When you look closely at the so-called 'democracies' of the West and the political systems of other regions of the world and you will be amazed that their *politics and politicking* are *not dirtier than their actual patterns of thoughts and life*. In other words, their politics and

politicking are as *stupidly-malicious and deranged* as the lives they live behind the (public) scenes and on the (public) scenes of their daily lives. So, *politics and politicking* can neither be cleaner or dirtier than the societies in which they are played or practised! That is a fact-based *Truth*. Check it.

[3] See Gospel of St. Matthew 5:14

[4] Sarcasm for *religionomists* (all marketers of religion) across the board it doesn't matter whether it is a Christian or an Islamic cleric or any other cleric from other religions.

[5] Sarcasm for the grossly insensitive politicians and their acolytes in government, they smile like doves but act like wolves. It doesn't matter whether they were once military personnel or life-long politicians.

[6] I am not sure, but I guess maybe they have done some things that they don't want anyone to know about, that is their current characters in the public sphere are not part of what they are in secret.

Chapter 11

The Destructive Effect Of God-Deyism

[1]There are different variations of this parlance.

[2] Psalms 145:18;10:17 and 25:3

[3] Religious, ethnic, traditional and socio-political affiliations

[4] Actively cooperating with *those divine energies* being showered on us through our prayers

[5] State of material *cum* physical indifference, especially one arising from the psychological withdrawal or noninvolvement of a person in his environment, which makes him look for external intervention to

solve (his or) societal (socio-political, economic, educational etc) problems.

[6] A defective psycho-spiritual state of *being* that requires a withdrawal from the world, a renunciation of the individual will, and reliance on God's/ divine intervention or decision in **everything.**

[7] Many people often blindly use letter St. Paul to the Romans 13:1-6 and other Bible passages to argue that it is God that chooses and sustains rulers. Yea, he does but he uses people –you and I. We aren't his robots, dummy.

[8] A series of actions directed toward a specific target, aim, objective or goal.

[9] 'Instinctive beings' are animals below human beings; they seem intelligent in the way they do things, build their 'houses' and 'manage' their lives and environments. Yet, there is nothing logical about their lives or actions.

[10] See Letter of St. James 2:18,19

Chapter 12

Mentally Lazy But Materially Greedy Generation

[1]Rampant intellectual fraudulence, dishonesty, illogicality or fallacy packaged as some genuine line of reasoning.

[2] Here, I am referring to people in their 25s, the 30s, 40s and 50 years, despite the increase their acquisition of higher certificates or educations.

The use of plural 'generations' instead of its singular form is deliberate; it's solely for contextual *emphasis*. Even though broadly speaking, they all fall into 'one younger generation', yet there are different generations within the younger generation itself.

[3] It is very common now to find 14 years old kids in SSS 3(which is not a bad thing) and 19/21 years in NYSC camps with first degree in the kitty, which is very good, or excellent.

[4] We are not even sure if it is hundreds of thousands or a million-plus since the state itself is semi-functional, and its agencies responsible for things like statistics of the population as whole and details of the varied sections of the population are either lame or 'dead' altogether.

[5] Information Technology involves processing and distribution of data using computer hardware and software, telecommunications, and digital electronics.

[6] A condition or a set of circumstances that allows or encourages or enhances the origin, development, or growth of something

[7]By 'mal-informed' I mean: we are orientated towards false expectation about life's processes, by manipulating facts to convince us to think *we now have the real knowledge,* while (in reality) we don't.

[8] By 'dis-informed' I mean: this generation (of youths) knows less because of the *tactful reduction* in the dissemination of the truth with the aim of supplanting the truth with (false pieces of) information that is neither *factual nor verifiable, thereby* making (us) the victims lose touch with ('sunny-day') reality. I mean our knowledge is somewhat half-baked with facts and fictions, and we are largely at fault.

[9] By 'uniformed': I mean we (this generation of young people) are not having the necessary awareness or the understanding of the facts as facts the way we should, or we are unable to interpret facts and sieve out (separate needed elements of information from useless details) the necessary knowledge from those facts. Put differently, this generation lacks basic education in *source validation or fact analysis* and knowledge absorption. Thus, in a particular sense, we are uneducated, unenlightened or ignorant all together in such context.

[10] "After all, what is education but a process by which a person begins to learn how to learn?" See Peter, Ustinov: Dear Me 1977 (Microsoft Encarta 2009). 1993-2008 Microsoft Corporation.

[11]My definition: *An educated person is someone who has learnt (how) to be a rational learner as well as being a practitioner of the knowledge acquired.*

Education, however, is a process that teaches you (how) to learn in both structured and random manners while practising the knowledge acquired; and also (it) incites you to practice logically and consistently while learning.

[12] This mindset is purely materialistic, it emphasizes the *titles* you have, the *positions* you occupy, whom you are *connected to*, etc.

[13] This mindset is rationally-moral, it emphasis the qualities that can build a just and equitable society, qualities such as integrity, sincerity, perseverance, courage, honesty, hardworking, selflessness, empathy etc

[14] Fa*c ti*on (pieces of fact + many fictions): government mixes ***huge*** lies with little truth.

[15] This refers to people who are *believed* to have the capacity to use *extrasensory perception* or the ability to get information via means other than sensory. Also included are people believed to have the ability to mentally move objects at a distance other than known physical forces "*psycho kinesis"*.

Chapter 13

Three "Most Successful" Industries in Nigeria

(Politics, Proliferation of Religious Houses and Clustered Prostitution)

[1] "272 firms shut down in one year –MAN," *Punch*, August 24, 2016, http://punchng.com/272-firms-shut-one-year-man/

[2] Well, I am not insinuating it is more rampant here than in other unserious countries around the world. I am only saying it is a shame that situations around the country are making people normalize an obvious aberration.

[3] One of them was Dr 'Basketmouth' Doyin Okupe, who was so successful that he served different administrations as their *attack dog* for almost 10 years. His last job was with the most *divisive president (Jonathan) of Nigeria* who was defeated on March 28, presidential election by a *random movement* for an *'unchanging but needed change'* symbolized by a weird 'austere' man (Buhari).

It was not necessarily the best change we needed then but it was the best time for a necessary change.

[4] One of these was a minister in the government of Jonathan that was defeated on March 28, 2015, presidential election. Of course, she was given a 'juicy government portfolio' and through her actions, she

proved to us that an idiot is always an idiot, notwithstanding her social status.

[5] Two of these are currently governors, one (Fayose) is currently ruling as anti-constitutionality and pro-impunity governor in northern-most part of Western Nigeria and the other one (Wike) is ruling in the core of south-south states on the rivers.

[6] Two of these were former governors of Bayelsa (Alamesiea) and Delta (I. James) states respectively.

[7] "Top Abuja Politicians Are selling their Lavish Houses to Fund Elections" New Nigeria, January 12, 2015, http://www.nairaland.com/2088996/top-abuja-politicians-selling-lavish

[8] "Exorbitant party nomination forms and systemic corruption," *Daily Trust,* Nov 13, 2014 https://www.dailytrust.com.ng/daily/columns/thursday-columns/39371-exorbitant-party-nomination-forms-and-systemic-corruption

[9] Kingsley Omonobi, "Offa Robbery : 4 Gang Leaders Accompanied Saraki To Sympathise With Offa Monarch –Police" *Vanguard Newspaper*, June 6, 2018, https://www.vanguardngr.com/2018/06/offa-robbery-4-gang-leaders-accompanied-saraki-sympathise-offa-monarch-police/

[10]For example Church of Wells in Texas: https://en.wikipedia.org/wiki/Church_of_Wells

[11] That is reaching out to fellow Christians of other denominations and letting them, 'the-would-be intra-converts,' see why they should join them instead of continuing with the other religious organization(s).

[12] Boko Haram wanted to establish an Islamic system at all levels of their to-be-established Caliphate, but poverty and police brutality fueled their warped ideological movement-turned-terrorist-organization more than any other factor.

[13] The ineptitude of the ruling elite became worst between May 2010 and May 29, 2015. And we are still trying to navigate our way out of it. Hopefully, the new government, starting from May 30th 2015 will initiate a new beginning.

[14] You are not asked to pay anything, but you will pay tithes if you want Jesus to bless you more. You need to pay something to support pastor's wellbeing; contribute your share of the development fee; support 'evangelization' drive and give 'Our Daddy and Mummy' in the Lord gifts of love etc.

[15] Muslim prayer group (or congregational worship centre) with configuration that is similar to the so-called Christian Pentecostal/independent worship communities. They usually have their name tags unique to them or their leaders.

[16] It is a simplistic *collection* of images, drawings, or 'write-up' or TV drama or audio recording that takes the form of a serious documentary but intentionally geared towards the ridiculing or mockery of its object(s).

[17] "The debacle of corporate prostitution in banks," *The People's Daily,* Nov 23, 2015 http://www.peoplesdailyng.com/the-debacle-of-corporate-prostitution-in-banks/

[18] Here, 'past' refers to their backsides and all the associated curves and the 'future' refers their chest/upper front section and all the associate cleavages

Chapter 14

Nigeria's Major 'Imperial' Elites

[1] Not all politicians are greedy or irredeemably corrupt, thus only those in politics for with aim of 'securing' life's pension are here referred to as the *ever-greedy*.

[2] It is a metaphor for undeserved and unjustifiable privileges.

[3] "Factbox: Nigeria's $6.8 billion fuel subsidy scam," *Reuter*s May 13, 2012 https://uk.reuters.com/article/us-nigeria-subsidy-graft/factbox-nigerias-6-8-billion-fuel-subsidy-scam-idUKBRE84C08N20120513.

[4] In an Al Jazeera interview with Aliko Dangote, he was asked again if he was granted exclusive right or privilege to import rice and sugar. Of course, you don't expect him to say it was true.

[5] "Aliko Dangote: Africa's richest man | Talk to Al Jazeera" *Al Jazeera English,* September 13, 2014, https://www.youtube.com/watch?v=XRBGX59O-gg

[6] In this instance the terrorists are oil marketers and their collaborators.

[7] In Yoruba language of Western Nigeria, if you are said to be richer than *sekere*, it means you have *an uncountable* money or you are stupendously rich. Though, *sekere* is musical instrument but it has a metaphorical meaning in Yoruba proverbs too.

[8] A leader like the former Nigeria president from May 10 2010 to May 29 2015

[9]An assemblage of cliques of conspirators or schemers, particularly one formed for political purposes.

[10] 'Balls' (testiculos duos) refers to any condition of the people that is highly critical.

[11]January 2012 national protests readily come to mind here, when almost all the pulpits were on holiday on the evil, malicious and spiteful festive period (December 25-31st) increase in fuel price by the inept *Jonathanian* government.

[12] Here pulpit refers to or means the clergy or minister of any or all of the major religious groups in Nigeria.

[13] See Letter of St. Paul to Timothy 6:6

[14] "CAN President, Oritsejafor, admits ownership of cash-stacked jet seized in South Africa", *Premium Times,* September 16, 2014 https://www.premiumtimesng.com/news/headlines/168224-can-president-oritsejafor-admits-ownership-of-cash-stacked-jet-seized-in-south-africa.html.

[15] Machiavellian here refers to a godless scheming, underhandedness, tricky, sneaky and cunning politics that seeks powers for callous reasons of any degree.

[16] Of course, *Quod erat demonstrandum* would mean, roughly, '*as demonstrated'*. But that is not what I mean; instead, I intend to say, 'at this moment I have said as much *as reality and reason* want me to say'.

Chapter 15

Errors of Political Parties in Nigeria

[1]"It is a closely organized system of beliefs, values, and ideas forming the basis of a social, economic, or political philosophy or program." See Microsoft Encarta dictionary 2009. (1993-2008 Microsoft Corporation).

[2] 'Hardwire' in computer conceptual framework means building a function into a computer with hardware rather than programming. Thus, I used it here to mean 'a solidly defined and accepted' political values.

[3] 'Symbols' are naturally deeper than 'signs,' so the logos of political parties should participate in the realities they try to reflect, unfortunately, political parties' symbols in Nigeria are best described as dead signs or *degraded signs* that lack the capabilities to be symbols. They mean nothing, just bunch of slogan-oriented nonsense.

[4] It is a very popular Yoruba word/slang and it means rosy or sweet or enjoyment-galore.

[5] Olumo Rock can be found in Ogun State in western Nigeria.

[6] Men and women behaving like people with an IQ of about 25 (see http://www.assessmentpsychology.com/iqclassifications.htm) or below and a mental age of less than 2 years 9 months old.

[7] An implicitly-directionless or template-less organization, that is open to all who feel pulled by or drawn to it, whether or not they understand what it claims to stand for; they just want to be a part of the group. Simply put, *Iruwa-ogiriwa* means a mindless mixture of different blends of locust beans.

[8]Just as it is in the military or paramilitary organizations, where candidates are informed about the 'dos' and 'don'ts' of such

organizations before joining them, so that once they go ahead and join any of those military organizations, they know the objectives, the dangers, and the honours of the organizations, and they know the dignity inherent in being loyal to the force to the end.

Therefore, since the candidates are fully aware of the philosophy of such organizations, they know they sign for whatever those organizations stand for -life or death, and they cannot be jumping from one military organization to another because such act will not be welcome quite easily.

[9] Objectively analyzing the characters and interests of every member and prospective members based on values and principles already established and say it the way it is irrespective of who he is or where he comes from.

[10]It's a reference to the cunning and peace-disrupting nature of the *malicious deception* perpetrated by the Biblical serpent of Genesis 3: 1-19.

[11] Sharing spoils of war was and is still a common motivating force (in and among rebels or renegade armies).

Chapter 16

Ethnocentric Pedestrianism of the Elites

[1]I mean call it what you like -lightweight, medium-weight or heavyweight; all of the weights put together are what I am referring to here. In other words, the middle class, upper-middle-class to the upper-class proper.

[2] Greek *bios* means life or way of living. *Stealth* means doing something slowly, quietly, and secretly, in order to avoid being discovered. The Greek words *sōma* = "body" and *sōmatikós* = "bodily" respectively.

Thus, *biostealthsomatic* therefore means living dishonest, or cunning life that the hides the real behaviors or actions of a person beneath subtle/gentle existence –like deadly bacterial on human skin. This, I should say, is a behaviour that conceals the real tricky, dishonest and dangerous life of somebody beneath a '*negligible surface existence'*. It is a kind of 'what you see is not what you get' existence.

[3] An ethnocentric psycho-political art of making (economic and political) tribalism so small, subtle and less detectable in an effort to give *it an appealing or negligible public existence* while still perpetuating its destructive evils.

Simply put, it is a psycho-political technique of hiding pervasive ethnicism behind every little excuse of justifying why a *specific group* of people deserves to have *this or that* 'right and privilege' while exploiting every other group, although the words 'right and privilege' are masterfully avoided when playing this psyche game on the public.

Note: The phrase '*ethno-nanopsychology of biostealthsomatic existence'* simply means (the *art of) concealing tribalism* beneath *negligible but dangerous existence.*

[4] I borrowed some theological undertones from Matthew 12:34 and 23:24

[5] It's a play on word, a metaphor. It means his fellow derided 'blacks' or African Americans.

[6] Modern in appearance but semi-primitive in approach.

Chapter 17

The Exit

[1] See Daniel 13:52; Amos 4:1; Exodus 22: 21-23; James 2:1-7 & 5:1-5.
[2] See Matthew 7:16

www.ingramcontent.com/pod-product-compliance
Lightning Source LLC
Chambersburg PA
CBHW021349210526
45463CB00001B/39

* 9 7 9 8 6 4 0 0 7 6 1 5 8 *